Contextual Teaching Works!

Helping Students Reach Higher Levels of Achievement

DALE PARNELL

CORD

Leading Change in Education

For additional copies, contact

CCI Publishing
324 Kelly Drive
Waco, Texas 76710
800-231-3015 or 254-776-1822
Fax 254-776-3906

Printed October 2000

ISBN 1-57837-278-x

CONTENTS

FOREWORD

Educators, parents, employers, and community leaders across the nation cry out for better learning opportunities for young people. In this book, Dale Parnell gives them the answer—contextual teaching and learning. Students seek meaning in what they learn, and learning becomes more meaningful when they see how the concepts they are learning are applied in life and work.

Basic academic subjects—mathematics, language, and science—become true tools for successful learning when they are learned in the context of their use. When the everyday application of concepts learned becomes apparent, the "ah-ha" moment of learning occurs and the concepts are integrated into the person's knowledge bank.

Because the mind seeks to make connections between what is known and new ideas, teaching concepts in the context of their use allows students to make those connections more easily and quickly.

- Math becomes meaningful when we can see how its concepts are applied in architecture, space travel, construction, and budgeting.

- Language becomes meaningful when we see its use in technical documents, great novels, newspapers, or a report for work.

- Science becomes meaningful when we can connect it to air travel, medical research, or understanding the way the universe works.

Contextual teaching has become a cornerstone of Tech Prep and has helped educators realize one the contributions Tech Prep makes to education reform.

In this book, Dale enlightens the reader about brain-based learning and the framework for contextual teaching and learning. He also provides proof, through research and case studies, of the value of contextual learning to student achievement.

The time you invest in reading *Contextual Teaching Works!* will offer a great return: useful knowledge about the way our minds construct learning and an understanding of contextual teaching and its value to enabling real learning to occur.

Darlene H. Blake
State Director of Tech Prep
Richmond, Virginia

ACKNOWLEDGMENTS

It's always difficult to write acknowledgments, since so many people contribute ideas, data, testimonials, and support, and there's always a danger of forgetting someone. However, I will try to list everyone who has been instrumental in the creation of this book, and offer my apologies to anyone I may inadvertently omit.

Initial thanks must go to Dan Hull, President and CEO of CORD, whose idea of putting qualitative and quantitative data about the effectiveness of contextual teaching and learning into the hands of educators was the catalyst for this book.

Next, my thanks to family, particularly my daughters, Sue Shields and Teresa Autry, my sons, Paul and Tim Parnell, and my son-in-law, Bob Shields, for their support and invaluable input, and also to my good friend Thomas Sticht.

My thanks also to Margaret M. Leary, President of CCI Publishing, for her initial edit of this book, and to Mark Whitney, Kay Liston, Helen Badley, and Virginia York of the CORD publications services department.

Next, my thanks to the following educators and students, who provided input for this book. Although some of it was not used in this edition, it was of great help to me and may be used in future editions or appendices to this edition. I appreciate the dedicated work that goes into educating our children, and I salute you for your efforts on their behalf!

Amy Pierson, Richmond High School, Richmond, Indiana

Beth Avery, Poinciana High School, Kissimmee, Florida

Bill Warren, Southern Maine Technical College, South Portland, Maine

Bob Thaden, Tacoma Community College, Tacoma, Washington

Chip Avery, Gateway High School, Kissimmee, Florida

Dawn Hahn, Pacific High School, Pacific, Missouri

Dennis Bruns, Camdenton High School, Camdenton, Missouri

Donna Murano, Olympia High School, Rochester, New York

Doug Dickston, Mt. Hood Community College, Gresham, Oregon

Ed Brady, Olympia High School, Rochester, New York

English faculty, New York City Technical College, New York

Jack Whittemore, Olympic High School, Charlotte, North Carolina

James Counce, Jemez Valley High School, Jemez Pueblo, New Mexico

Jesse Mase, Southern Maine Technical College, South Portland, Maine

Joanne Langabee, Papillion LaVista High School, Papillion, Nebraska

Jo Ann Crow, Gadsden High School, Gadsden, Alabama

Joel White, Lexington High School, Alabama

John Geubtner, Tacoma Community College, Tacoma, Washington

Judith Miller, Worcester Polytechnic Institute, Worcester, Massachusetts

Judy Edwards, Ragsdale High School, Jamestown, North Carolina

Kathy Jo Elliott, Workforce Alliance, Carrollton, Georgia

Ken Tunstall, *If I Had a Hammer,* Big Spring, Texas

Larry Fernandez, Sweetwater High School, National City, California

Leslie Cash, Shelby County High School, Columbiana, Alabama

Linda Graham, Pawhuska High School, Pawhuska, Oklahoma

Linda Smith-Staton, Pellissippi State Technical Community College, Knoxville, Tennessee

Linda Williams, Sapulpa High School, Sapulpa, Oklahoma

Lisa Bogaty, Pellissippi State Technical Community College, Knoxville, Tennessee

Maggie Chadwick, Southern Maine Technical College, South Portland, Maine

Mary Lindquist, former President of National Council of Teachers of Mathematics

Mary Shelton, Cape Girardeau Central High School, Cape Girardeau, Missouri

Melinda (Mindy) B. Hester, Laurens District 55 High School, Laurens, South Carolina

Michelle Green, Stringer Attendance Center, Stringer, Missouri

Nancy Smith, School Board of Sarasota County, Florida

Nan Glen, Dunwoody High School, Dunwoody, Georgia

Nickolyn Russell, Hillsboro R-3, Hillsboro, Missouri

Pam Fails, Lexington High School, Lexington, Texas, who was instrumental in gathering much information from other educators

Pam LaGasse, Sarasota County Technical Institute, Sarasota, Florida

Pat Wilder, Fitzgerald High School, Fitzgerald, Georgia

Pat Grasso, Blue Hills Regional High School, Canton, Massachusetts

Patty Arnall, Christian County High School, Hopkinsville, Kentucky

Ronald Cheetham, Worcester Polytechnic Institute, Worcester, Massachusetts

Richard Barton, Jemez Valley High School, Jemez Pueblo, New Mexico

Sharlette Martin, Morris High School, Morris, Oklahoma

Sydney Rogers, Nashville State Technical Institute, Nashville, Tennessee

Teresa Rollins, CORD, Waco, Texas

Wylene N. Wilks, North Sand Mountain High School, Higdon, Alabama

CHAPTER 1

WILL THIS BE ON THE TEST?

We have a real dilemma in education! The contemporary demands upon teachers, particularly teachers in elementary and secondary public schools, are mammoth and often unrealistic. Time constraints and political pressures often force teachers to choose between what they know is good teaching and their survival as teachers. The current testing craze aimed at requiring students to pass state-mandated standardized tests places even greater pressure on teachers to emphasize less-than-effective approaches to teaching and learning. These and other pressures will probably further entrench traditional pedagogies that have little relationship to how the human brain really works, the ways individuals learn best, and the development of higher levels of student achievement.

The traditional "sit and listen" approach to teaching might well be called the "freezer method" of education. In this method, knowledge is handed out to students, who are told to put it into their mental freezers so they can thaw it out later should they ever need it. A minority of students can handle theoretical and abstract teaching; the neglected majority of students fail to see much meaning in what they are asked to learn, so they memorize it only well enough to pass some kind of test. That is why students often ask their teachers, "Will this be on the test?"

Another question that students almost always ask teachers is, "Why do I have to learn this?" The familiar reply has been, "Because you might need it someday." Even the most cursory look at the majority of reports on student educational attainment and achievement reveals that large numbers of students are not finding this a very satisfactory answer to a good question. Too often they are not learning to solve real-life problems or to function as effective citizens in our democracy. Many times, they are not even acquiring the content they are told they will need someday.

Oregon has established some of the most rigorous legislatively mandated education testing programs in the country. Students must pass a battery of academic tests at grade 10 to earn the Certificate of Initial Mastery and be able to go on to earn the Certificate of Advanced Mastery at grade 12. However, little investment has been made in teacher professional development or in changing teaching methodology in the classroom. After several years, Oregon now has the highest high school dropout rate of any state in the union. Nearly one third of students who started in the Portland-area high schools four years ago failed to graduate with their class of 2000 because they dropped out, flunked out, fell behind, or just left school because they were bored to tears.

Few things in education are more dehumanizing and more certain to generate difficulties in the schooling process than for students to see their education as a meaningless experience. Yet, too often we allow just that to happen, particularly for that neglected majority of students who are unlikely to earn four-year baccalaureate degrees. For these students, when meaning is lost, hope is lost. Soon, they are lost.

Population Changes

The school population has changed dramatically over the past 100 years, as shown in Figure 1, below. In 1900 only about 6 percent of the 17-year-old population were high school graduates. By 1930 this proportion had risen to 29 percent, and by 1950 it had grown to 59 percent. The percentage of graduates peaked in 1970 at about 76 percent and dropped to 73 percent in 1990. The National Center for Education Statistics is predicting that the percentage of high school graduates will fall even more this year, to about 70 percent (*Digest of Education Statistics,* 1999, 26–27).

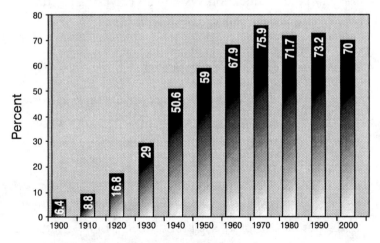

Figure 1. Public High School Graduates as a Percentage of the 17-year-old Population

One possible reason for this decline is that many students who opt out of high school take the General Educational Development (GED) test. This is an alternative method of gaining equivalency credit for high school. The number of students earning the GED diploma has nearly doubled over the past thirty years, from 227,000 in 1971 to over 500,000 in 1999. The GED Testing Service, operated by the American Council of Education, estimates today that one of every seven students who have completed the requirements for high school holds a GED credential.

These statistics alone should tell us that the school teachers of 2000 are facing a much different student population than the teachers of 1900 faced. Today we are attempting to deal with a vast array of individual student differences: in intelligence levels, in family and economic background, in cultural background, and in the ways people learn. Over the past one hundred years we have moved into a universal and mass education system, endeavoring to educate all kinds of people with all kinds of diversity.

New Wine, Old Wineskins

It makes for interesting cocktail-party conversation to ask individuals of my generation—people above the age of 65—how much schooling their parents had. In my case, my father left formal school after the third grade, while my mother completed the eighth grade. My very unscientific polling of older citizens finds a similar educational pattern among the parents of today's senior citizens. In my lifetime I have moved from cow chips, to potato chips, to computer chips—growing up on a farm and experiencing the *agricultural age,* moving to the city and experiencing the *industrial age,* and then moving into our current *technological age.*

This should make us realize how radically our environment has changed in a relatively short time. Perhaps our major problem with education reform efforts today is that we are working with an educational system and teaching methodologies designed for another demographic time with other cultural and economic conditions. We have been endeavoring to put "new wine" into "old wineskins." When that happens, the wineskins burst, the wine runs out, and the wineskins are ruined. This biblical analogy describes what is happening to education today. The "new wine" of education reform is being tested and evaluated using the "old wineskins" of traditional teaching methodologies.

Despite huge population changes in schools over the past one hundred years, as illustrated in Figure 2, the teaching process has changed very little. We continue to use traditional teaching methodologies and the industrial model of standardized time periods for grading.

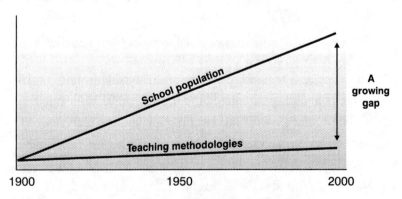

Figure 2. The Growing Gap Between Changes in Student Population and Changes in Teaching Methodologies

---

In the mid-1980s, Vito Perrone, a professor at Harvard University, led a team of scholar-educators in a high school visitation project for the Carnegie Foundation for the Advancement of Teaching. Fifteen high schools representing diverse locations, sizes, communities, social classes, and racial distribution were involved in intensive observation. One of the most pungent observations to come out of these visitations had to do with traditional teaching:

> Structurally, curriculum appears very much as it has been for most of the last fifty years. . . . There is a sameness about how teachers approach their teaching. The format is fairly conventional, textbook oriented, information filled. . . . We saw very little inquiry teaching, and problem-solving skills did not tend to be taught. (Perrone, 1985, 645–50)

In addition to the sameness of teaching observed by the Perrone group, we still adhere to something called the Carnegie unit, which was developed about 85 years ago. At that time there was confusion about what a high school transcript of credits really meant for university and college officials. To rectify that situation, the Carnegie Foundation proposed a standard unit, based on time, to measure high school work. A total of 120 hours in one subject, with class meeting four or five times a week for 40 to 60 minutes for 36 to 40 weeks a year, earns the student one unit of high school credit. The Carnegie unit has become a standardized way of measuring student academic progress. To this day, this time-structured system forms the basis for organizing the high school curriculum and the school day. For many students, learning seems secondary to adding up the seat time required to earn Carnegie units.

If we are to effect education reform, we must realize that educational institutions do not exist in isolation from the economic, social, and cultural situations that sponsor and surround them. The current debate about education reform almost totally ignores the tremendous population shifts and structural changes in our society, as well as the vast individual differences in the mass of students in schools today.

> **Educational institutions do not exist in isolation from the economic, social, and cultural situations that sponsor and surround them.**

Think about it! In the course of the twentieth century we had one major war that introduced the use of the airplane and the reality of bombs falling from the sky. Then we had a second major war, during which the atomic bomb was introduced to blow up entire cities. Today we can travel into space and experience instant communication around the world. What would life be like for the young people of today if the inventions of the past one hundred years were to disappear? Imagine a world without automobiles, telephones, airplanes, computers, televisions, air conditioning, and cell phones. Yet, despite these inventions—which have changed our world and work radically—most students sit in classrooms and experience teaching much as students did around 1900.

Life Changes

To understand how radically our lives have changed, we have to look at how my generation and my parents' generation lived. To work on the farm you didn't punch a clock and go to do one task repetitively. Instead, you generally worked from sunrise to sundown and, in the process, experienced many different things.

To accommodate the agrarian economy, school calendars provided a long summer vacation from school so that students could help out on the farm. Most students completed only eight years or less of schooling, and most of their knowledge was gained from a few books and whatever knowledge the teacher could convey to them. Thus, students were rich in experience but poor in knowledge.

Today, students are in a totally different environment, one that leaves them rich in knowledge but poor in experience. In an information-rich age, where and how do they gain the experience that they need to apply knowledge?

In the early years of the twentieth century, America was moving from an agricultural economy to an industrial economy. This meant that families were moving from rural areas to urban centers to fill the abundant industrial jobs that were becoming available. Immigrants were also coming to our shores in search of better jobs and better lives, and, to them, education was particularly important.

Factory work at the turn of the twentieth century turned out to be the opposite of farm work. The daily regimen of the industrial factory started with a whistle and ended with a whistle. Individuals in the factory specialized in doing the same tasks over and over again, with little communication occurring with other workers. Problems were referred to managers, rules and regulations were clearly spelled out, and the workday was centered around time worked.

Educational institutions were asked to accommodate the growing population. Unfortunately, schools adopted the same time-structured, time-defined factory model of operation. However, they kept the long summer vacation left over from the agricultural age. The school day started with the bell, and students moved from time-structured subject to subject, specializing in one subject at a time and experiencing traditional theoretical and abstract teaching. With rare exceptions, that is the way schools are still organized today.

Educational Changes

In the 1996 national political campaign we heard the slogan "It's the economy—stupid!" Our contemporary slogan for education reform should be "It's all about teaching—stupid!" Yet, the political pundits of today seem to say we need more of the same, which will now be measured by some type of standardized testing system. Whatever else educators do, they cannot change the school calendar, and they must see that kids sit and listen quietly in classrooms for six hours a day. It seems as if educators can have all the innovation they want as long as it does not change any of the time-honored traditions and expectations of education.

Obviously, change in education does not happen easily. When salutary changes are recommended, educators immediately bump their collective heads against the reality of political agendas and parental expectations. It seems that the education reform rules are clear! You can change anything in schooling except the school calendar, the time-structured school day, or the teaching process in the classroom. Thus, the way we have organized ourselves for education reform has little to do with the ways students learn. Until we move education reform into the classroom and match our organizational structures with the ways people learn, we will continue to work on the fringes of real reform with small gains in student achievement.

> The way we have organized ourselves for education reform has little to do with the ways students learn.

Since 1982, American education has undergone the most intense scrutiny in history. If reports and political rhetoric alone could improve student learning, we would have certainly achieved excellence in education during the 1980s and 1990s. But most of the reform reports and much of the political rhetoric seem to center on a fourth "R"—reporting. The emphasis has been on achieving accountability through standardized testing—testing that has little application to real-world issues. It's as if administrators and legislators are thinking, "Let's find out what students know or don't know and identify the teachers who are culpable for their not knowing."

A good problem to examine is the issue of mandated statewide testing. Look at a couple of typical test items that students must answer to earn the Oregon Certificate of Initial Mastery and ask yourself, "What kind of teaching will prepare all students (not just some students) to answer this kind of test question?"

Eighth-Grade Reading Test: "Tasaku"

Read this story of the stonecutter Tasaku, a man who wished to be powerful, and then answer the questions.

Tasaku, a lowly stonecutter, worked at the foot of a mountain. He was happy with his work until one day a noble prince went by in a magnificent royal procession. Tasaku wished aloud for such great wealth, and the spirit who lived in the mountain heard him.

Tasaku was transformed into a wealthy and powerful prince. He walked happily through his gardens until one day the sun burned his flowers and they wilted. Tasaku realized that the sun was more powerful than a prince, and he asked the mountain to turn him into the sun.

Tasaku became the sun and, to show his power, he burned the fields and parched the lands. The people begged for water. Then a cloud came and covered his bright rays. Tasaku saw that the cloud was more powerful than the sun, and he told the spirit to change him into a cloud.

Tasaku became a cloud. With his new powers he made violent storms. Fields flooded; huts and palaces washed away. But the mountain remained. Tasaku was furious. "Make me into a mountain!" he demanded. The spirit obeyed and then departed, for he could do no more.

Tasaku became the mountain and was more powerful than the prince, the sun, and the cloud. But Tasaku felt the sharp sting of a chisel. It was a humble stonecutter chipping away at his feet. Deep inside, he trembled.

1. What kind of writing does the story of Tasaku seem most like?
   a. A short story
   b. A fable
   c. A tall tale
   d. A newspaper article

2. Sometimes an author makes something happen differently from what the reader expects. In literature this is called "irony." When in the story of Tasaku do you see irony?
   a. When Tasaku is a mountain and a stonecutter begins chipping at his feet
   b. When Tasaku made violent storms and flooded the fields
   c. When Tasaku demanded that the spirit make him into a mountain
   d. When the spirit who lived in the mountain heard Tasaku and made him a prince

Tenth-Grade Math Test

The figure below is formed from unit cubes.

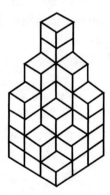

Contextual Teaching Works!

The three faces of the figure that you cannot see are solid—no cubes are missing. What is the volume of the figure in cube units?

a. 27 cubic units
b. 31 cubic units
c. 33 cubic units
d. 35 cubic units

Without making value judgments about the legitimacy of these test items, I wonder what percentage of adults could correctly answer them. I also wonder whether students can see the real-life application in these kinds of test items. What teaching methodology will best prepare a student to answer these test items correctly?

Take Learning Out of the Freezer!

Unfortunately, teaching decisions have traditionally been made on the basis of an instructional hierarchy whereby students must first gain facts and subject matter content and then, much later, learn to apply that content. Yet many teachers are beginning to see the limitations in this stair-step view of teaching. Educational theorists and cognitive scientists are suggesting a different pattern for teaching and learning, in which *acquiring* knowledge and *applying* that knowledge occur interactively. Master teachers observe that, when students are actively engaged in applying new knowledge, higher levels of achievement can be gained (Applebee, 1989).

We have often heard of individuals quoting someone, or some writing, out of context. Unfortunately, many teachers are trained to present knowledge outside the context of its application. Thus, students are required to commit bits of knowledge to memory in isolation from any practical, real-life application.

The glaring omission in most of the how-to-fix-it reports and most of the political rhetoric has been a lack of emphasis upon teaching and learning—the central mission of education. The simple fact is that a teaching methodology that worked for the small percentage of the population in school 100 years ago does not work well for the much larger percentage in school today.

To gain some insight into this problem, consider these questions:

> **The simple fact is that a teaching methodology that worked for the small percentage of the population in school 100 years ago does not work well for the much larger percentage in school today.**

- Will more of the same lecture-and-test teaching increase student achievement? Will it prepare a world-class workforce?

- Will more of the same classical content-centered (and contextless) teaching lower the high school dropout rate?

- Will more of the same theoretical teaching help the mass of students to become better connected with real-life problem-solving issues?

The two basic tenets of contextual teaching—that context just as important as content and that context may determine whether the content has been mastered—should be obvious. Both are essential and must be inextricably linked in the teaching and learning process.

There is really no teaching methodology worthy of the name "new," and contextual teaching is no exception. Good teachers throughout history have placed strong emphasis on helping students see meaning in their educational experience. They have motivated students by relating knowledge to the practical realities of daily life, and have encouraged students to learn through hands-on practical experience. I even venture to say that, because contextual learning is so deeply rooted in the way the human brain is designed to work, where substantial learning has taken place, contextual teaching principles have been at work.

It was the work of William James, a 19th-century physician, philosopher, and psychologist, that gave contextual teaching its most solid foundation. "No reception without reaction, no impression without correlative expression," was the rule that James espoused for teachers. James urged teachers to help their pupils put new knowledge to immediate use—to help them build up useful systems of combining knowing with doing. However, James died at a relatively young age, and his teachings and research have been largely forgotten.

With rare exception, teacher-training institutions continue to turn out future teachers who think they must give students content about 90 percent of the time, with maybe 10 percent of the time spent on application and learning for meaning. Those teachers who do try to increase student achievement by making their instruction a balance of content and context are hampered by the perceptions of many. These include some school system leaders, community leaders, and parents who regard experiential, activity-centered learning as an add-on rather than the backbone of the learning experience.

In contextual teaching, it is the major task of the teacher to broaden students' perceptions so that meaning becomes visible and the purpose of learning immediately understandable. This is not an add-on or something nice to do. It is fundamental if students are to be able to connect knowing with doing. In summary, contextual teaching is an educational philosophy and teaching methodology that focuses on enabling students to find meaning in their education.

> **It is the major task of the teacher to broaden students' perceptions so that meaning becomes visible and the purpose of learning immediately understandable.**

After 50 years in education, I am convinced that few other teaching strategies will so effectively help increase student achievement as helping students make the connections between classroom subject matter and the real-life challenges they will face throughout their lives. Connecting the "why" of concrete reality to the teaching process provides an essential motivational force for learning. If students are to be motivated to learn, they must see and feel the touchstones of reality and meaning in their educational experiences.

Works Cited

Applebee, Arthur, Judith Langen, and Ina V.S. Mullis, *Crossroads in American Education*. Princeton, N.J.: Educational Testing Service, 1989.

Boyer, Ernest, *High School: A Report on Secondary Education in America*. New York: Harper and Row Publishing, 1983.

Digest of Education Statistics, Washington, D.C.: National Center for Education Statistics, 1999.

Perrone, Vito, *Portraits of High Schools*. Carnegie Foundation for the Advancement of Teaching, Princeton University Press, 1985.

A nation that draws a broad difference between its scholars and its warriors will have its thinking done by cowards and its fighting done by fools.

Thucydides

CHAPTER 2

TEACHING THE WAY INDIVIDUALS LEARN BEST

Contextual teaching is not watered-down instruction. It is simply teaching the way individuals learn best—helping students make connections between their lives and the knowledge and information they are discovering. This ability to make connections gives the student a touchstone of reality upon which to build solid and meaningful learning.

It is vitally important that educators fully understand the breathtaking power of the human brain to make meaningful connections between knowledge and the application of that knowledge, between knowing and doing, and between content and context. On the down side, it is also vital for educators to understand the limited power of the brain to deal with material that does not connect. The brain is designed to perceive patterns and make connections, and it resists having meaningless information thrust upon it.

Since the brain tends to discard information for which it finds no connection or meaning, many students find their education meaningless. They then drop out because their brains will not allow them to repeat meaningless learning over and over. Is it any wonder that one out of four of our public school students does not complete his or her high school education?

A computer, like a teacher, can supply knowledge and information, but it cannot help students make connections between their lives and that knowledge and information. It is the major task of the teacher to help students make connections so that the purpose of learning is immediately understandable.

Connecting students with reality is especially important in view of the distorted versions of reality that our modern-day culture tends to promulgate. Television and computer games are prime culprits in this regard, with hours of programming that present wealth and sex as the keys to happiness and violence as the key to getting your own way. Such programming offers a world of questionable values and instant gratification, with heroes and heroines who are always attractive and never responsible for their actions.

While examples of human selflessness and courage abound, these examples are not often noticed or celebrated. Have we as a country used our wealth and our technology to create thickets of unreality that stand between us and the real issues of life? Have we in education allowed there to be a gulf between academic and vocational education and between knowledge and the application of knowledge?

No longer can the debate about the importance of academic education over vocational or career and technical education be allowed to degenerate into an either/or argument. They are both important, but, unfortunately, we have allowed a wide gap to exist between the two.

The basis for contextual teaching is combining information-rich subject matter content with experience-rich

Contextual Teaching Works!

contexts of application. This means that academic and vocational-career and technical education are interrelated and can contribute much to the teaching process.

Does "Academic" Mean "Better"?

Public opinion in the United States has generally followed the line of thinking that academic education is the most important type of education. The corollary assumption is that vocational education is inferior. The opinion still exists across the country that there are some individuals who work with their heads and some who work with their hands. This is out of line with reality and the way the human brain functions.

Can it be that our problem in teaching contextually is a problem bigger than just education? Adults and children alike often seem disconnected from some of the most important realities of how our democratic society must function. The connectedness issue runs through our homes and communities, as well as our schools. Ernest Boyer, the late president of the Carnegie Foundation for the Advancement of Teaching, related a story to me a few years ago:

> When I was the U.S. Commissioner of Education (now called the Secretary of Education), Joan Cooney, the brilliant creator of *Sesame Street,* came to see me one day. She said she wanted to start a new program at Children's Television Workshop on science and technology for junior high school kids, so they could better understand the real world. (It was subsequently

funded and called *3-2-1 Contact*.) In doing background work for that project, Cooney and her colleagues surveyed some junior high school kids in New York City, and asked such questions as, "Where does water come from?" A disturbing number said, "The faucet." And when they asked, "Where does light come from?" students answered, "The switch." And when they asked, "Where does the garbage go?" students answered, "Down the chute."

The sense of connectedness for these students went as far as the television set, the refrigerator door, the light switch, and the garbage chute.

What is the greatest sin committed in our schools today? In my judgment, it is the failure to help students use the magnificent power of the brain to make the connections between:

- knowing and doing
- academic and vocational education
- schooling and other life experiences
- knowledge and the application of that knowledge
- one subject matter discipline and another
- subject matter content and the context of use

The Brain and Learning

The process of what is now called "brain-based learning" calls for making these connections. Psychologists, philosophers, and educators from William James to John Dewey to Jerome Bruner—all the way to Howard Gardner and Robert Sternberg of the current time—have made the

---

case for making connections in education. In the past couple of decades, neuroscientists have shown the need for making connections in the teaching and learning process, and this process is rooted in the basic functions of the brain itself.[1]

The human brain is a marvelous biological instrument consisting of many interconnected parts. Functionally speaking, the brain can be described as having three major parts: the brain stem and cerebellum, the limbic system, and the cerebrum.

The smallest part of the brain consists of the brain stem and the cerebellum; we can think of this as the automatic-reflex brain. The brain stem controls automatic body functions like breathing and heartbeat. The cerebellum controls muscular activity and balance.

The limbic system, which surrounds the upper brain stem, is composed of the hippocampus, the thalamus, the hypothalamus, and the amygdala. The hippocampus plays a large role in memory-related learning, the thalamus relays information from the senses to the cerebral cortex, the hypothalamus largely controls sexual urges and other motivations, and the amygdala mostly controls anxiety and fear. The limbic system primarily controls short-term memory and, through a process that is not completely understood, transfers selected information to the long-term memory in the cerebrum, which fills the entire upper part of the skull.

---

[1]   For more on brain-based learning, see Eric Jensen, *Brain Based Learning*, Turning Point, 11080 Roselle Street, San Diego, California, 1995.

The cerebrum, the most remarkable part of the brain, can truly be called the thinking brain. It controls our language development, our thoughts, and our voluntary actions, and stores our long-term memories. In short, the cerebrum makes us human. It contains about three-quarters of the 100 billion neurons in our brain. A pinhead-size part of the cerebrum can house 30,000 neuron cells. These neurons hold the key to the brain's efficient system of communication and of making connections.

We can get a sense of this fantastic communication system by considering how the neurons "talk" to each other. Neurons communicate with each other by releasing several kinds of chemicals, called neurotransmitters. An individual neuron receives messages from other neurons and, based on the strength of the electrical signals that excite the neurotransmitters, "decides" to pass the message along.

The neurotransmitters pass to other neurons over tiny gaps called synapses. The synapse contact points—which number in the thousands—are on tree-like fibers called dendrites, which are the branching arms of the neurons that transmit and receive messages. What is interesting about this complexity is that new synapses tend to accumulate as the brain acquires new information and new experiences. Thus, our brains create neural networks and maps as we gain experiences. When no connection to an experience can be found, or when the neurotransmitter impulse is very weak, a message is not sent to other neurons.

The Effect of New Experiences

Judging from experiments with animals, new experiences that activate certain parts of the cerebrum seem also to make the neurons grow fuller and richer. Their cell bodies become larger and their dendrites develop new branches on which to accept additional connections with other cells. Thus there seems to be a direct relationship between enriched environments, life experiences, and brain development (Diamond, 1988, and the Society for Neuroscience, 1993).

Educators know from experience that students change both physically and psychologically as they grow and gain experience. Educators also know that students from enriched home environments seem to have increased ability to learn. It seems reasonable to hypothesize that the physical structure of the brain can change as a result of experience, and that an educational environment that is as rich in experience as it is in information can have a positive impact upon learning.

> **Educators know from experience that students change both physically and psychologically as they grow and gain experience.**

Every time an individual achieves something or experiences something that connects with a previous experience or perceived meaning or value, that achievement or experience will tend to "stick"—and something will be learned. The reverse of this is true for experiences or information that do not connect or hold perceived meaning.

Here is a little test to illustrate the point of making connections:

Try memorizing a group of unconnected nonsense words like:

cre   *bli*   *ret*

Then try memorizing a group of unrelated words like:

chair   *water*   *light*

Now try memorizing a group of related words like:

money   *shopping*   *bargains*

Finally, try memorizing this part of a sentence:

Beverly went shopping for bargains . . . .

We quickly realize that each group is easier to remember than the one before it. This illustrates the point that there is little inherent meaning in instructional material alone. Meaning comes from making a connection, and the more instructional material can be made meaningful for the student, the more easily that information can be assimilated into the cerebrum. The more easily it can be assimilated into the cerebrum, the easier it will be to associate that information with future problem-solving issues.

These observations about brain-based learning can have profound significance for teaching. For more students to achieve higher levels of learning, they must be motivated to acquire the *content* of knowledge along with the *context* of application, and thus develop the ability to solve problems and to assimilate and associate that knowledge in a way that can be useful in new situations.

Based on various contemporary theories of how the brain functions when we are endeavoring to learn something,

I have come to believe that the brain responds differently to different stimuli. For example, a timed test may cause a student to downshift in his or her use of the brain. Fearing the possibility of failing the test or receiving a low grade, the student will tend to call upon the short-term memory (limbic system) rather than the thinking brain (cerebrum).

Unfortunately, the current political rush to statewide standardized testing will, in too many cases, push students to use their short-term memories and allow their thinking brains to rest. This is a reasonable response, because most standardized tests call on short-term memory.

The Learner Becomes a Problem Solver

The challenge of contextual teaching is to keep alive in our students their natural tendencies toward active, problem-solving learning. One can only wonder where in the teaching and learning process we have lost this. When I observed the early years in the development of our children and grandchildren, I saw that they handled things, explored, knocked down, set up, put together, crawled, walked, talked, and imitated. Yet, in the schooling process, particularly in the upper grades and in college, the primary teaching process emphasizes the passive learning methods of looking, sitting, listening, and memorizing.

Whatever else we are as humans, we have an innate desire for meaning. This need to find meaning is a strong motivational force in all our lives. If teachers can consistently help students see meaning in their education via contextual teaching, I think we will be astonished at the increase in the achievement of more students.

It is important to note that I am not trying to convey a feeling that all classroom experiences must be fun for meaningful learning to take place. The teaching and learning experience is not just a bottle of happiness pills. Also, expectations of student performance should not be lowered to the lowest common denominator. But, insofar as is possible, all teaching should be aimed at being meaningful for the students so they use their brains' larger capacity to make the connections between content and context.

Contextual Teaching Framework

At this point it might be helpful to recall the contextual teaching framework that forms the model for brain-based learning:

- *Learning for acquisition of knowledge.* Students acquire knowledge and, to retain it sufficiently, they apply that knowledge to some real-life situation.

- *Learning for application.* Students are actively engaged in the processing of knowledge and performing authentic tasks to gain an understanding of how to use knowledge.

- *Learning for assimilation.* Students demonstrate sufficient understanding of knowledge, and the application of that knowledge, to make the connections to new learning and new situations.

- *Learning for association.* Students learn to transfer acquisition, application, and assimilation of knowledge to new problem-solving situations.

If education reform is to move beyond the margins, some fundamental and systematic changes must be made in the ways we approach the teaching and learning process. Whether we call it "contextual teaching," "situated cognition," "active learning," "experiential learning," or "constructivist teaching" matters little. What does matter is that many educators carry the torch for teaching the way students learn best.

Works Cited

Boyer, Ernest, unpublished paper. Princeton, N.J.: Carnegie Foundation for the Advancement of Teaching, 1991.

Diamond, M., *Enriching Heredity: The Impact of Environment on the Anatomy of the Brain*. New York: Free Press, 1988.

Jensen, Eric, *Brain Based Learning*. Turning Point, 11080 Roselle Street, San Diego, California, 1995.

Society for Neuroscience, Brain Facts, 11 Dupont Circle, Washington, D.C., 1993.

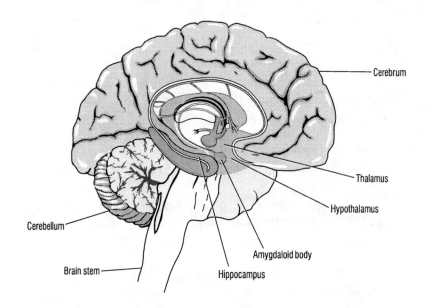

The Amazing, Interconnected Brain

CHAPTER 3

BARRIERS TO HIGHER STUDENT ACHIEVEMENT

The educational enterprise and its related teaching methodologies have remained largely unchanged over the past 100 years. We use standardized tests and textbooks that do little to connect learning with how the brain really functions. We have a standardized system of grading periods and semesters that does not recognize the vast individual differences in student learning speeds or learning styles in the typical classroom of today. We have a "cover the material" mind-set that largely ignores whether students have learned or not. We have an unrealistic image of excellence in education. We have an unconnected educational process that continues to ignore continuity in learning. These standardized approaches and teaching

> The educational enterprise and its related teaching methodologies have remained largely unchanged over the past 100 years.

methods have in many ways become the jail from which contemporary pedagogy has been unable to escape.

The Time Barrier and Student Achievement

Probably the greatest barrier to implementing active learning and teaching contextually is the commitment of the educational establishment, at all levels, to time-defined and time-structured organization. Educational institutions from kindergarten through graduate school continue to operate on a system of semesters or quarters, with time-certain grading periods, traditional school hours, and a lengthy summer vacation so students can do farm work that no longer exists.

In the vast majority of educational organizations, time is the constant and student competence the variable. The amount of time a learning task should take is predetermined—like sand in an hourglass. Students have only as much time to complete a given assignment or task as it takes for the sand to run out of one end of the hourglass.

Probably the greatest challenge to changing educators' views of the relationship between time and student achievement is the constant pressure on teachers to cover more and more material in a given time period. Many teachers fear, with good reason, that active learning—which is integral to contextual teaching—will not allow time to cover a given amount of material within a limited amount of time. This perceived need to cover the material presses teachers and students alike to fall back on the assembly-line approach of industrialized mass production that has remained unchanged for many years.

The most widely used system of time-structured standardization is the high school Carnegie unit, which was described in Chapter 1. The Carnegie unit is based more on seat time than on competence, and represents an 85-year attempt to codify learning. It would be great if the Carnegie system could be transformed into a system based on units of competence rather than units of time. But that transformation is unlikely until the stranglehold of standardized units of time is broken in education.

The current school system of hours and semesters can be called "the 6-9-12 problem for educators"—six hours a day, for nine months, for twelve years. All students are expected to learn whatever schools have to offer within a given time period. If a student cannot learn what he or she is expected to learn within that time period, that fact is noted on the student's permanent record as a failing or low grade, which remains there forever. This paradigm may be applicable to assembly-line production, but it is not applicable to a modern-day educational process that recognizes the reality that individuals learn at different speeds.

Our current time-bound educational system seems to sort most students on the basis of those who learn within an arbitrary time allocation and those who do not! To reinforce this time allocation system, some teachers grade on the curve rather than for mastery, and test experts develop norm-based standardized tests.

Here are a couple of pertinent questions related to the use of time in education. How many students do you know who are exactly nine-month learners, or 18-week-semester learners? How many students do you know who are exactly 12-year learners? One can only wonder whether student achievement could be improved if some students were given a little more time and if they could go over the learning cycle a few more times. What are we doing to a student who may be a ten-month learner, or for that matter a seven-month learner?

Today, assembly-line education, which is a relic inherited from past generations, is a significant barrier in the struggle to meet the diverse educational needs of an increasingly diverse population. Any serious attempt at education reform—that is, any attempt that places learning and improving student achievement at the heart of the effort—must reverse the traditional relationship between time and competence. Competence must become the constant and time must remain the variable. Of course, other elements in the contemporary educational institution form barriers, but changing education's time-bound approach to learning is critical.

> **Competence must become the constant and time must remain the variable.**

We now know that experiences and environment shape the development of our brains and therefore impact the ability of our brains to learn. Contextual teaching, active learning, and experiential learning take time and usually cannot be squeezed into a 50-minute class period or a nine-month school year.

The jury is still out regarding the extent to which experience affects brain development. However, any veteran teacher has observed that, when students are exposed to enriched home lives over time, their ability to learn increases. Since experience impacts the structure of physiological organs of the body, it is reasonable to hypothesize that the physical structure of the brain, which is also a physiological organ, can change if given time to gain appropriate experience. Allowing sufficient time to gain experience for brain development is particularly critical for students from impoverished homes. Far too many students from these homes remain low achievers and do not complete their high school experience when subjected to a time-driven assembly-line kind of education.

Here are a few diagnostic questions to ask about your educational organization as related to the use of time in the teaching and learning process:

1. Is student competence the constant and time the variable in your organization? If not, why not?

2. Are all of the students in your school 18-week learners? (Eighteen weeks is the length of a typical semester.) Could it be possible that there are some 16-week and some 20-week learners in your school?

3. Is it possible that some of your students who are now labeled "average" or "below average" could increase their levels of achievement given the opportunity, and some support, to go over the learning cycle a few more times?

4. When the sand runs out of one end of the hourglass, is learning over for your students?

5. Which of the following approaches will increase achievement for more students?

   a. Give a final subject matter exam and a final grade based on what has been learned in a fixed time period

b. Test on how a student can apply learning to a problem-solving situation, then use the test results to determine what still needs to be learned and give some extra time to develop mastery of that needed learning

What approach is used in your school or college?

6. Does your school grade students on the basis of learning within a given time period, or are grades given on the basis of subject matter mastery?

7. Can you identify what stands in the way of changing the time-structured organization in your institution?

8. In your judgment, will "more of the same" traditional teaching and time-structured organization produce higher levels of achievement for more students?

In many graduate schools, the faculty members grade students on the basis of an "A" or "B" or "C" grade or an "incomplete." The incomplete remains on the student record until the student can master the material and complete the course. If this policy is good for helping graduate students be successful and meet high standards, why wouldn't it, or some policy like it, be good for all students at all levels of education?

Are we interested in simply sorting students, or are we interested in helping more students gain higher levels of achievement?

> Are we interested in simply sorting students, or are we interested in helping more students gain higher levels of achievement?

Covering the Material and Student Achievement

Another of the great barriers that inhibit teaching for meaning is the pressure to cover the material. Most teachers really want to teach for meaning, but there is always the fear that active learning—which connects subject matter content with real-life experiences—will not allow enough time to cover all the material in the textbook. The perceived need to cover a certain prescribed amount of knowledge presses students and teachers alike to fall back on stuffing information into the mental "freezer," rather than developing active thinking and connected learning.

Textbooks often determine the content to be covered in a given class, and most modern textbook publishers operate on the basis that more is better. More information is being revealed every day, and they feel they must keep up. Unfortunately, very little material is ever deleted, and teachers feel compelled to cover the material. To add to their stress, they must do this within the constraints of a system of hours and semesters mandated by their institutions.

This results in a persistent tension in teaching—between covering an increasing volume of knowledge (whether students learn it or not) and doing so within fixed time periods that have changed very little over the years.

Many teachers fear, with good reason, that contextual and applied teaching will not allow time to cover all the material that will be on standardized tests. And, since their teaching effectiveness is frequently determined by how well their students do on such tests, they forsake teaching in the ways the brain learns best. In fact, the standardized testing movement pushes hard for the "cover the material" approach to teaching and defies rational observation about how the brain really operates when individuals try to learn. It certainly promotes the assembly-line approach to education.

Standardized tests do little to connect subject matter with real-life applications, or to evaluate whether students can use their learning to solve problems or see things in the mind's eye—both vital competencies for long-term success. We are only now beginning to understand how little standardized tests do to improve student achievement. Rather, they are more likely to tell us more about the socioeconomic makeup of the community a given school serves.

Faulty Images of Excellence and Student Achievement

Consider for a moment the image of excellence in education that most people have. Is it a picture of "smart" kids who perform well on verbal or mathematical tests and then go on to four-year colleges where they excel in traditional liberal arts studies, go on to graduate school, and then enter professions such as law, medicine, or even education?

If it is, we need to ask ourselves how reasonable a scenario this is for most students. Given that only about 25 percent of the adult American population actually hold four-year baccalaureate degrees (according to the latest census), this image of excellence is reasonable for only a relatively small number of students—those whose intelligence leans toward the linguistic or the mathematical and who learn easily in abstract and theoretical modes.

We certainly want excellent doctors, lawyers, accountants, engineers, and teachers. But what about the rest of the population? Could it be possible that policemen or nurses with associate degrees or aircraft technicians might also be considered excellent? Of course it is. I know that, when I fly on an airplane, I want the aircraft technician who prepares the craft for flight to be excellent.

If only 25 percent of adults hold baccalaureate degrees, it seems reasonable to say that about three out of four students in the public schools will probably never earn four-year college degrees. Of course, this figure can change from community to community, based on socioeconomic conditions, but are we as a nation prepared to write off a large majority of the students because our definition of excellence is too narrow?

We need to give this thoughtful consideration, since many institutions of higher education define excellence beginning with the admission process. This is designed to screen out students who don't measure up to specific criteria. Obviously, an institution can ensure excellence if its entrance scores are high enough. In this way, excellence is determined by who gets in! But, does such a system really define excellence, or does it simply sustain a system for sorting out students who do not quite fit the traditional image of excellence?

There is nothing inherently wrong with tough admission standards, if that is part of the mission of a given institution. But what *is* wrong is for institutions with tough admission standards to be viewed as the *only* educational institutions of excellence. Other definitions of success must be accepted. Public schools and community colleges, for example, work on the basis of a not-so-visible definition of excellence called "student success." These institutions do not test students to screen them out, but to screen them in—into an experience that is conducive to success. These schools and colleges must focus on "value-added" excellence or academic progress. They must ask, "Where was this student upon entry, and how well has he or she progressed?"

A pervasive and unrealistic image of excellence in education has led parents, teachers, administrators, and even students to celebrate only one kind of excellence, leaving many other students feeling like failures.

I visited the office of the superintendent of a large school district on the west coast and observed college banners from Harvard, Yale, and similar colleges and universities all around his office. When I asked where the banners from the surrounding community colleges were, he said that his school district "was making a great effort to promote excellence, and nearly anybody can get into a community college." It was obvious that this educational leader had only one definition of excellence, and it was based on who gets into a four-year college or university.

> A pervasive and unrealistic image of excellence in education has led parents, teachers, administrators, and even students to celebrate only one kind of excellence, leaving many other students feeling like failures.

When visiting high school guidance counseling offices, I rarely see banners from the local community colleges or banners celebrating apprenticeship opportunities. I can only wonder whether these high schools have concluded that there is only one kind of excellence and that the students who do not live up to it are somehow second rate.

The point of this discourse on excellence is that what we honor as excellence in education drives, in part, the priorities that teachers develop for their teaching. If there is only one definition of excellence—the college prep-baccalaureate degree curriculum—that perception diminishes all other kinds of teaching and the neglected majority of students who will not ever gain baccalaureate degrees. The goal of contextual teaching is to help all students feel successful and to increase their achievement.

The goal of contextual teaching to help all students feel successful and to increase their achievement.

One of the most pressing dilemmas for educators is to develop a working criterion of excellence that fits the great range of individual differences among students—whether rich or poor, black or white, academically able or "challenged," or destined for a university or for a specific job. The variety of student aspirations and the multiplicity of socioeconomic and cultural backgrounds and experiences require multiple definitions of excellence.

Social and educational status must not be a substitute for equality of opportunity and individual achievement in any curriculum or any field of study. It will not serve our democracy well if a single definition of excellence becomes a cover for a retreat from concern for equity and opportunity. An educational institution that provides the same pedagogical approaches for all students and the same time frame for learning for all students cannot honestly make the claim of pursuing excellence.

Improving Student Achievement

The Rand Corporation recently released a study entitled "Improving Student Achievement: What National Assessment of Educational Progress State Test Scores Tell Us." The Rand study did not get into classroom teaching or the operation of local schools but concentrated on which state-level policies deliver the biggest educational payoffs. It concluded that the policies that make the most difference in student achievement are (1) reducing class size in the early grades, (2) making preschool widely available, and (3) ensuring that teachers have the up-to-date classroom materials and in-service training they need.

What is striking about this study is the conclusion of the researchers—that good test scores primarily reflect the advantages the students bring to the formal schooling process. The socioeconomic makeup of a community or state strongly influences how well students do on the NAEP (National Assessment of Educational Progress) tests.[1]

---

[1] The Rand report was reviewed in *The Oregonian*, Portland, Oregon, on July 27, 2000; the NAEP tests are the closest thing the United States has to national achievement testing.

**Table 1. Excellence in Education:
Images Versus Realities**

Illusory Images of Excellence	Realities of Excellence
One classical school curriculum will meet the needs of all students.	Students need structure and substance in their school programs, but these must be presented in context so students can see the application of their learning.
All students learn at approximately the same speed.	There are vast individual differences among students of any age in speed of learning and comprehension of knowledge.
All students must learn the basic skills by the elementary grades.	Development of basic skills must be placed on a continuum of learning, with students arriving at different points at different times. Excellence in education requires breaking the lockstep of arbitrary time requirements for learning.
The traditional classical textbook and lecture method of instruction is the most effective approach to teaching for most students.	Some students learn rapidly by one method of instruction and more slowly under a different approach. However, contextual teaching and learning appear consistently more effective than classical instruction.

Illusory Images of Excellence	Realities of Excellence
Real excellence can be found only among those students and programs related to the pursuit of baccalaureate degrees.	Some new definitions of excellence are needed. Excellence is just as important to the aircraft technician as to the engineer, to the secretary as to the business professor. Every school and college program must develop standards of excellence, and the goal of excellence must be held up for every course and every student.
Covering the subject matter material is more important than gaining a depth of understanding. Education becomes a mile wide and an inch deep.	Depth is more important than breadth in helping students gain understanding. Instead of concentrating on covering the textbook, teachers should select material to help students understand the application of key knowledge.

Excellence in teaching and learning cannot be pursued as we would chase an elusive butterfly. It certainly cannot be achieved by sorting and labeling students. Excellence will happen and student achievement will increase for all as we cultivate the educational soil with some new teaching approaches that match how we teach with how the human brain functions. True excellence in education must be an excellence that is achievable for individuals of all races and all cultural and socioeconomic backgrounds.

Learning Fragmentation, Poor Attendance, and Student Achievement

One of the disappointing aspects of the major reports on how to "fix" American education is the scant attention given to continuity in learning. Students in most schools and colleges go from subject to subject, from grade to grade, and from school to school with little sense of continuity or connection.

For the most part it is left up to the student to grasp that the use of mathematical formulas might be helpful in an applied physics class, or that English lessons on clear written communication might apply to a written report in health occupations. Most students have little sense that one class builds on another or that their education is preparing them for real-life situations.

The tremendous mobility of contemporary American society also contributes to the loss of continuity in learning. An estimated 25 to 30 percent of public school students attend more than one public school each year. A lot of people move from town to town or from state to state. Given this reality, it is amazing that students who belong to highly mobile families learn as much as they do. Public school teachers do the best they can to take students where they are in a given learning cycle, but, with heavy class loads and demands from other students, the time needed to deal at any length with the mobile student is limited.

Irregular class attendance also contributes to a loss of continuity for students. It has been estimated that, in some large urban high schools, as many as 30 to 40 percent of the students are absent on any given day, particularly Mondays and Fridays. When students miss a significant number of classes, it is difficult for them to feel a sense of connectedness and to work to their potential. It is a fairly safe bet that student achievement would increase dramatically for some students if their class-attendance patterns improved.

Students miss class sessions for many reasons, but the one that should bother educators most is student boredom. When students see how what they are learning relates or connects to something in real life, they become active, interested learners. Thus, teachers who consistently use contextual teaching methodologies indicate that one of the most notable effects is the improvement in student attendance.

As one high school chemistry teacher told me:

> After teaching high school chemistry for 32 years with modest success, I was ready to hang it up. Then I discovered applied chemistry (called *ChemCon*). I now have students waiting at my door in the mornings to get into the chemistry lab. I have never had this much fun teaching chemistry. What is interesting, I am now getting all kinds of students in my chemistry classes, not just the university-bound kids. . . . I am going to continue to teach a few more years.

Loss of Continuity and Student Achievement

Unfortunately, teachers in American schools and colleges work in relative isolation from each other. This leads to a loss of continuity between high schools and colleges. Some of this loss can be attributed to the widely decentralized nature of our educational system, which inhibits effective communication. But, even in situations where high schools and colleges are in close proximity to each other, there is little communication about the real "stuff" of education—teaching and learning. When communication does happen, it is not usually about preparing lesson plans or ensuring continuity of learning.

One of the obstacles to teacher communication is the problem of time. When teachers teach all day, every day of the school year, little time is left for cooperative planning. Preparing contextual lessons that require student involvement and the application of learning is a time-consuming proposition and often requires teamwork—and teamwork is foreign to most teachers. Professional development days and activities are often considered a frill by school boards and, when planned by administrators, viewed as busy work by teachers.

Even the physical setup of the facilities provided for teachers presents a barrier to good communication about teaching and learning. Teachers keep their teaching plans and materials in their own classrooms or, in colleges, in their private offices. The only common space where they can meet is usually a cramped room with a few chairs and a coffee machine.

Do High Standards Alone Really Improve Student Achievement?

In promoting the higher-standards movement across the country, the goal of politicians and educational leaders should be increased achievement for more students. But, before they can reach that laudable goal, these leaders must realize that students learn at different speeds and that the very structure of the current educational system works against such increases.

It is the responsibility of leaders at all levels of education to challenge the current barriers to higher levels of student achievement. Higher standards are only half of the equation; the more important half is the design of teaching methodologies and programs that help students meet those higher standards.

Higher standards are only half of the equation.

There are at least three options for helping students reach higher standards:

1. We can give all students the same college prep curriculum and have them all experience the same teaching methodology in the same time periods. We can fail those who do not memorize well, do not think well in the abstract, do not do well on timed tests, or do not see the usefulness of what they are being asked to learn. This remains the option of choice in many educational institutions today.

2. We can "dumb down" our teaching and make our standardized approaches easy enough for nearly all our students to succeed. Instead of examining our teaching methods, we can water down the subject matter content and grade more leniently. We can fill the students' mental toolboxes with fluff rather than equipping them for lifelong learning.

3. We can examine the barriers that prevent us from teaching for meaning and connectedness, and change our teaching approaches. Increasing student achievement

does not require lowering standards, but it does require an understanding that all students will not meet the standards in the same time frame. It does not mean teaching different subject matter; it means teaching subject matter differently.

I am reminded at this point of a conversation I had with a concerned high school principal. He related to me that he had discovered that more than 400 of his 1200 students had received one or more failing grades the previous semester. In his musing about this discovery, he wondered whether the students were at fault or the school was doing something wrong. His next comment was telling:

> We are trying to pursue excellence in this high school. We have high standards and tough courses. We are proud of how many students we place in "good" colleges and our large number of merit scholarship winners. I guess we just cannot expect our non-college-bound students to do well in our higher-level academic courses.

Clearly, the third option—the teaching for meaning option—will increase student achievement and open the door to excellence for more students. In the next chapters we will examine some exemplary practices that should convince us of this premise.

Of course, this cursory analysis of some of the barriers to higher student achievement will not satisfy individuals who are convinced that all students should experience the same teaching methodology and be measured by the same time-structured grading periods. However, this observation does suggest an intriguing tongue-in-cheek possibility. Why not just limit the pool of students taking the SAT and ACT college entrance examinations to the top academic 25 percent of a given high school student body? Or, why not ask some students to stay home on the days the tests are given?[2] Test scores would rise dramatically. Political leaders could then be proud of the quality of our schools, and the media could report on the great improvements in education.

Works Cited

Rand Corporation, "Improving Student Achievement: What the National Assessment of Educational Progress State Test Scores Tell Us." *The Oregonian*, July 27, 2000.

Note: Some of the information and interviews cited in this chapter were developed from the research done for Chapter 4 of my book *Why Do I Have to Learn This?* which was published by CORD Communications, Inc. (now CCI Publishing) in 1995.

---

[2] Recent news reports suggest that this is actually being done in some schools!

Contextual Teaching Works!

What Research Says About Contextual Teaching and Higher Levels of Student Achievement

The armed services of the United States are the nation's largest employers of young adults. They also operate the largest education and training programs in the nation. Even though they have an unusually strong advantage in terms of control of individuals, there is much we can learn from the military's education and training experiences. After all, the armed services face many of the same problems as public schools: There are large differences in ability among individuals, and these must be accommodated.

The military finds it just as difficult to educate and train individuals of widely varying aptitudes as public schools do. For example, the military has found that slow learners require two to five times as much individual instructional time as faster learners. It has also found that slow learners learn best when they *apply* information as they learn it.

(Public school teachers also know this, but various factors in public education prevent them from using application as a fundamental teaching principle.)

Educators at all levels of education can learn from the military's research: Knowledge and information are best learned if the context is meaningful to the individual and if learning connects to some realistic and recognizable application. This should bolster the confidence of those who want to provide meaningful education for their students, since they know contextual teaching is a solid principle.

Competence is built on the confidence that comes from understanding, and understanding comes from seeing the application of knowledge. It is abstract and theoretical teaching with which most individuals have the greatest difficulty.

The military has concluded that "front-loading" the literacy education and training process with abstract knowledge acts as a barrier to effective military job training. People do not need to acquire specific levels of learning before they can start learning the skills needed to move into a job. The acquisition of reading, writing, and mathematics knowledge and skills is best accomplished by understanding the functional context of a job.

The military has also concluded that teaching basic skills and training skills together reduces the time spent in training. Integrating education and vocational teaching—doing what the military calls "functional context education"—improves learning.

> **The military has concluded that teaching basic skills and training skills together reduces the time spent in training.**

Teaching Low-Aptitude Individuals

In 1987 a team of cognitive scientists and educators published a book entitled *Cast-off Youth: Policy and Training Methods from the Military Experience*.[1] This book reports on a two-year study, funded by the Ford Foundation, that reviewed some 40 years of research and development in literacy and training programs used by the military. The study concentrated on individuals in the military who are generally considered to be on the low end of the aptitude section of military selection tests.

We can learn much from this study because it gives us the largest database in the nation of what can be considered the education and training of "at-risk youth." Military human resource research laboratories have pursued the improvement of literacy related to job training (functional literacy education). To create "functional" education means to make the learning more meaningful through practical application. In other words, contextualizing learning.[2]

During World War II, the military began to study the literacy needs of low-aptitude personnel. The order was given that literacy teaching was to be functional and related to military life. Because the literacy efforts of that era in the military were focused upon a very narrow body of military

---

[1] Thomas Sticht, William Armstrong, Daniel Hickey, John Caylor, *Cast-off Youth: Policy and Training Methods from the Military Experience*, New York: Praeger Publishers, 1987.

[2] What is most interesting about this research in military literacy education is the coining of the phrase "functional context education" by researcher Thomas Sticht.

content and because the time allotted for teaching was limited to about three months, the evaluations of those efforts are very mixed.

The Vietnam-era military gave additional emphasis to literacy education, but this time the approach was changed to a functional context approach. The content to be studied was not about military life in general, but about specific job content. In follow-up research, the functional context, job-related literacy approach was compared to the traditional general literacy programs that the Army was already using. The job-related and contextualized literacy efforts were evaluated as showing much greater improvement in job-related reading over general literacy programs.

That alone is an important finding, but even more important was the finding that the troops experiencing the job-related literacy programs did not see themselves as getting "remedial work," but rather as getting "job training." In terms of self-esteem, this finding has profound implications for educators at all levels of the educational process. Individuals tend to act out the labels that have identified them as slow learners, remedial learners, or "just plain dumb." If you ever hear anyone say, "I am just dumb at math!" you should realize that this is a self-fulfilling prophecy, acted out over a lifetime.

> **Individuals tend to act out the labels that have identified them.**

Unfortunately, many educators miss the point that education is not something that one gets first and learns to apply later. The military has found, in terms of training, that people who have experienced the front-loaded, education-first training do not do as well as people who experience contextualized education and training together.

The military research outlined in *Cast-off Youth* was, by and large, limited to literacy and vocational training programs. However, there is much to be considered in this research. In the special projects in which functional context education methodologies were followed, the teaching and learning process was judged to be more effective than traditional teaching for all levels of aptitude, and unusually effective for lower-aptitude individuals.

Table 2 outlines eight special military projects that used functional context education methods in teaching military recruits over a 50-year period. The researchers concluded that functional context education is beneficial across the aptitude spectrum.

> **The researchers concluded that functional context education is beneficial across the aptitude spectrum.**

It is important to observe that, as cited in *Cast-off Youth*, in all of the experimental military programs aimed at functional context education, individual achievement was improved, and in many cases improved substantially. Also notable about the military research is the sheer number of participants.

The Army's experimental contextual teaching course program in electronics field radio repair established during the 1954–1960 period involved 200 people with limited aptitude in both traditional and contextual classes. The individuals experiencing functional context teaching had higher test scores and overall improved achievement.

This was the first formal military experiment with the functional contextual education method. The performance of 100 students who had completed the contextual course was compared with that of 100 graduates of the traditional Army course. Individuals who completed the contextualized course were found to be "significantly superior" to those who completed the traditional course.

Table 2. Experimental Military Projects: Using Functional Context Teaching Methodologies[3]

Project	Service	Reduce Attrition	Reduce Time in Training	Improve Achievement
Basic electricity and electronics (average aptitude)	Navy	Yes	Yes	Yes
Electronics (low aptitude)	Army	Yes	—	Yes
Field radioman class (average aptitude)	Army	—	—	Yes
Electronics technician course (average aptitude)	Navy	—	Yes	Yes
Medical corpsman (average aptitude)	Army	—	—	Yes
Radio operator course (limited and average aptitudes)	Army	Yes	Yes	Yes
Project 100,000 (limited aptitude)	All services	Yes	Yes	Yes

---

[3] Sticht, *Cast-off Youth*, p. 98.

Project 100,000

During the Vietnam War, Secretary of Defense Robert McNamara initiated a controversial program to bring 100,000 lower-aptitude and marginally literate personnel into the military service as part of the War on Poverty effort of the Johnson administration. Needless to say, this initiative was roundly opposed by many of the leaders in the armed services and dubbed by some, "McNamara's Moron Corps." There was then, and still is today, a universal opinion that lower-aptitude individuals cannot or will not learn.

Secretary McNamara insisted on implementing Project 100,000, and insisted that this project should collect a massive amount of data, carry out related research analysis, and establish good control groups for comparison purposes. He saw this effort as a "controlled experiment" in the education and training of disadvantaged personnel in the military. It was his premise that these products of the "culture of poverty" could benefit from the education and training offered by the military. But who was right—the critics of Project 100,000 or Secretary McNamara?

As it turned out, McNamara was right! The results indicate that, while Project 100,000 personnel, when considered as a group, did not achieve as well as the higher-aptitude comparison group, this does not reveal the whole story. What is omitted is where these individuals started. The astounding finding is that the large majority of Project 100,000 individuals—75 to 95 percent—were rated "good" or "highly effective" in their job performance by first-line military supervisors.

But how did they do it, and what were the methods used to help this low-aptitude group make such improvements?

The Project 100,000 management team developed a functional context approach to the education and training of these personnel.

Five basic education and training principles were followed in the operation of the project:

1. Literacy education was integrated into technical training. (Context)

2. Insofar as possible, teaching was related to specific military situations. (Context)

3. Specific course objectives were designed to be contextual and job related. (Context)

4. Areas of learning difficulty were identified (like time needed to learn), and the practices were revised. All personnel in Project 100,000 were given extra time, extra help, after-hours study time, and learning repetition as needed. (This is certainly an element of contextual teaching.)

5. All initial instruction was related to what the individuals already knew, taking them from the known to the unknown, rather than the reverse. (Contextual teaching)

It is interesting to note that Project 100,000 veterans, when compared with a nonveteran group of similar backgrounds, earned more per hour, achieved more education, and had less unemployment. Sixty-eight percent of Project 100,000 veterans used the GI Bill.

The information from Project 100,000 presents researchers with a gold mine of material to analyze. Unfortunately, it has not been generally available for civilian personnel to review. As a result of the Project 100,000 research, other military projects have confirmed that functional context education can improve learning.

In 1971 the U.S. Army adopted a literacy training program that integrated literacy education with job training. Effectiveness data collected from over 3,000 military personnel revealed that improvements in all cases were greatest among those experiencing the integration of literacy education with job training. As a result of this effort, the federal government's General Accounting Office recommended to Congress that literacy education in the military be integrated with job training—which means contextualized.

In 1977 the Navy initiated a Job-Oriented Basic Skills Program (JOBS) with the primary purpose of improving the achievement of lower-aptitude personnel in technical training. The program was designed to feature functional context education methodologies in the teaching process. Of the 1,500 JOBS graduates studied, 1,200 had gone on to higher levels of technical training.[4]

SCANS Research

Dr. Tom Sticht, President and Senior Scientist of Applied Behavioral & Cognitive Sciences Inc., and his colleagues deserve much credit for their analysis of the military projects.

---

[4] It is also interesting to note that the military generally has the same bad practice as civilian educational institutions: separating the functions of education and training. This practice always presents organizational barriers to contextualizing and integrating academic with vocational education. But, even with this barrier, we can learn much about how experimental military programs that featured contextual teaching improved student achievement.

These can be found in the book mentioned earlier, *Cast-off Youth*. Based on his research with the military projects, Dr. Sticht was able to help convince the Secretary of Labor's Commission on Achieving Necessary Skills (SCANS) to include an emphasis on contextual teaching in its mission statement.

SCANS was formed in 1989 under the leadership of then Secretary of Labor Elizabeth Dole and Assistant Secretary Roberts Jones. Representatives from business, industry, labor, government, and education (including this writer), labored mightily to shed light on the question, "What does work require of schools?" This then became the title of the first Commission report.

The Commission staff studied the cognitive science research literature related to the importance of contextual teaching. They also interviewed a number of cognitive scientists and more than 500 private and public employers to discover what they expected of educational institutions and what kind of education and training they thought would be required to meet future needs. As a result of the extensive research, interviews, and discussions, the Commission formed the following mission statement:

> We believe that these skills (SCANS-recommended skills and competencies) are best learned in context and especially in the context of realistic workplace problems. Thus the teaching of functional skills will require the most radical change in educational practices since the beginning of this century. (SCANS 1991)

A set of recommendations was boiled down to a three-part foundation—basic skills, personal qualities, and thinking skills—and a five-part set of competencies that employers wish schools would foster in future workers. (See Tables 3 and 4.)

Table 3. SCANS-Recommended Foundation Skills and Workplace Competencies[5]

Foundation Skills
Competence requires:
Basic skills: reading, writing, arithmetic, mathematics, speaking, and listening.
Thinking skills: thinking creatively, making decisions, solving problems, seeing things in the mind's eye, knowing how to learn, and reasoning.
Personal qualities: individual responsibility, self-esteem, sociability, self-management, and integrity.

Workplace Competencies
Effective workers can productively use:
Resources: allocating time, money, materials, space, and staff.
Interpersonal skills: working on teams, teaching others, serving customers, leading, negotiating, and working well with people from culturally diverse backgrounds.
Information: acquiring and evaluating data, organizing and maintaining files, interpreting and communicating, and using computers to process information.
Systems: understanding social, organizational, and technological systems, monitoring and correcting performance, and designing or improving systems.
Technology: selecting equipment and tools, applying technology to specific tasks, and maintaining and troubleshooting technologies.

---

[5] Secretary's Commission on Achieving Necessary Skills, United States Department of Labor, "What Work Requires of Schools," Washington, D.C.: U.S. Government Printing Office, 1991.

Table 4. Contextualizing SCANS Competencies into Core Curriculum Areas[6]

Competency: RESOURCES	
English/ Writing	Write a proposal for an after-school career lecture series that schedules speakers, coordinates audiovisual aids, and estimates costs.
Mathematics	Develop a monthly family budget, taking into account expenses and revenues, and—using information from the budget plan—schedule a vacation trip that stays within the resources available.
Science	Plan the material and time requirements for a chemistry experiment, to be performed over a two-day period, that demonstrates a natural growth process in terms of resource needs.
Social Studies/ Geography	Design a chart of resource needs for a community of African Zulus. Analyze the reasons three major cities grew to their current size.
History	Study the Vietnam War, researching and making an oral presentation on the timing and logistics of transport of materials and troops to Vietnam and on the impact of the war on the federal budget.
Competency: INTERPERSONAL SKILLS	
English/ Writing	Discuss the pros and cons of the argument that Shakespeare's *Merchant of Venice* is a racist play and should be banned from the school curriculum.
Mathematics	Present the results of a survey to the class, and justify the use of specific statistics to analyze and represent the data.

---

[6] Secretary's Commission on Achieving Necessary Skills, U.S. Department of Labor, *Teaching the SCANS Competencies*, Washington, D.C.: U.S. Government Printing Office, 1992, ISBN 0-16-037908-3.

Contextual Teaching Works!

Science	Work in a group to design an experiment to analyze the lead content in the school's water. Teach the results to an elementary school class.
Social Studies/ Geography	In front of a peer panel, debate whether to withdraw U.S. military support from Japan. Simulate the urban planning exercise for Paris.
History	Study America's Constitution and role-play negotiation of the wording of the free state/slave state clause by different signers.
Competency: INFORMATION	
English/ Writing	Identify an abstract passage from a novel to support an assertion about the values of a key character.
Mathematics	Design and carry out a survey, analyzing data in a spreadsheet program using algebraic formulas. Develop table and graphic display to communicate results.
Science	In an entrepreneurship project, present statistical data on a high-tech company's production/sales. Use a computer to develop statistical charts.
Social Studies/ Geography	Using numerical data and charts, develop and present conclusions about the effects of economic conditions on the quality of life in several countries.
History	Research and present papers on effects of the Industrial Revolution on class structure in Britain, citing data sources used in drawing conclusions.
Competency: SYSTEMS	
English/ Writing	Develop a computer model that analyzes the motivation of Shakespeare's *Hamlet*. Plot the events that increase Hamlet's motivation to avenge the death of his father by killing Claudius.
Mathematics	Develop a system to monitor and correct the heating/cooling process in a computer laboratory, using principles of statistical control.

Science	Build a model of human population growth that includes the impact of the amount of food available on birth and death rates, etc. Do the same for a growth model for insects.
Social Studies/ Geography	Analyze the accumulation of capital in industrialized nations in systems terms (as a reinforcing process with stocks and flows).
History	Develop a model of the social forces that led to the American Revolution. Then explore the fit between the model and other revolutions.
Competency: TECHNOLOGY	
English/ Writing	Write an article showing the relationship between technology and the environment. Use word processing to write and edit papers after receiving teacher feedback.
Mathematics	Read manuals for several data-processing programs and write a memo recommending the best programs to handle a series of mathematical situations.
Science	Calibrate a scale to weigh accurate portions of chemicals for an experiment. Trace the development of this technology from earliest uses to today.
Social Studies/ Geography	Research and report on the development and functions of the seismograph and its role in earthquake prediction and detection.
History	Analyze the effects of wars on technological development. Use computer graphics to plot the relationship of the country's economic growth to periods of peace and war.

Contextual teaching and learning formed the underlying premise of the SCANS recommendations. This Commission was unanimous in its belief that, in the classrooms of America, learning to *know* must be integrated with learning to *do*. Commissioners were also quick to acknowledge that classrooms must be places for learning and not simulated worksites. Still, examples from the world of work can represent the touchstones of reality for nearly everyone, bringing life to the content of knowledge.

Contextual Teaching Research in High School Settings

Applied Mathematics

The contextual approach to teaching and learning is not a new pedagogical method. There have always been highly effective teachers who motivate their students to achieve academically by connecting content to context. One of the first educational tools for teaching mathematics contextually was called *Applied Mathematics*—now *CORD Applied Mathematics*—developed in 1986–1988 by a consortium of 40 state education agencies led by CORD. *Applied Mathematics* was developed as an alternative to the remedial general mathematics courses, which taught few if any algebra skills. It was designed as a two-year course for high school students who struggle with math taught abstractly. The contextual approach pioneered by *Applied Mathematics* is successful in both academic achievement and student motivation.

The first large-scale test of *Applied Mathematics* was administered during the 1992–1993 school year— 326 students completing *Applied Mathematics* at 20 schools in 13 states were tested in algebra 1 concepts and compared to 843 traditional algebra 1 completers.[7] The results showed no significant difference between the mean algebra test scores of the two groups, despite *Applied Mathematics* students' significantly lower entry-level skills.

During the same school year, four researchers from the University of Georgia studied the *Applied Mathematics* curriculum as it relates to college preparatory credit.[8] One of their findings dealt with the motivational impact of teaching contextually:

> Thirteen of the eighteen teachers report a very high rate of student success, grades of B and A, in *Applied Mathematics*. They attribute this success, with students who have not previously been successful in mathematics, to the positive attitudes students have toward the material and the activity-oriented approach to teaching as opposed to direct instruction and practice. Twelve of the eighteen teachers cited the relevance of the curriculum as a factor in engendering positive student attitudes.

Student motivation is best described by the students themselves. The following are excerpts from students' end-of-course critiques:

> I have learned more in this class than I have in any other math class I've been in. Since this is a "hands-on" course, it's more understandable and a lot more

---

[7] Candace Todd, "A Report on the Attainment of Algebra 1 Skills by Completers of *Applied Mathematics 1* and *2*," CORD, July 1993.

[8] William D. McKillip, Edward J. Davis, Thomas R. Koballa Jr., and J. Steve Oliver, "A Study of *Applied Mathematics* and *Principles of Technology* Relative to the College Preparatory Curriculum Final Report," University of Georgia, July 1993.

enjoyable. I am comfortable working with my classmates in groups and asking questions, as before, I was very shy and afraid to ask questions.

I can now understand and work out almost any story problem, whereas before I hated and could not do story problems at all!

It is important to be able to have a group work together toward a common goal. I hated math with a passion before I took this class and my past grades reflect it. I know that I will use this later and that gives math a sense of purpose for me.

It's better with the group effort from everybody helping you. Some were better at something than others.

The best part of this class is that you get to work in a group. So you learn more. In other math classes, you just sit there.

It takes longer to understand, but once you get it, it's pretty easy.

CLIC Project

The Contextual Learning Institute and Consortium (CLIC) was a funded U.S. Department of Education Innovation in Education project, sponsored by the School of Education at Oregon State University during the1995–1996 school year. The project had as its prime objective the establishment of a consortium of professional educators in five urban high schools in Portland, Oregon. The purpose of the project was to experiment with contextual teaching methodologies in a variety of subject matter settings. The high schools were chosen partly on the basis of having teachers with interest and some experience in contextual teaching and partly on the basis of the interest of the high school principals in leading the teams of academic and vocational teachers.

A summer institute for consortium members was held preceding the project. This institute provided teacher training in contextual teaching and allowed the gathering of teacher and expert opinions on contextual teaching. The impact of this methodology on student accomplishment and attitudes toward learning was also evaluated to determine the effectiveness of the contextual teaching methodology.

The project was organized around the formation of a contextual teaching team in each high school, with the high school principal as the team leader. Thirty-two teachers and 350 students enrolled in 15 different subject areas, from freshman English to junior physics, were involved in the project. No seniors were involved in the project, since follow-up work in the next school year was anticipated. Each high school developed an eight-person team composed of six academic and two vocational teachers. Quarterly dinner meetings held by the project director brought all the teams of the five high schools together for interaction and reporting on progress and challenges.

> **The project was organized around the formation of a contextual teaching team in each high school, with the high school principal as the team leader.**

For the project, contextual teaching was defined as the integration of academic and vocational education, or the combining of content with the context of application in the core subjects of mathematics, English, sciences, and social sciences. In September of 1995, faculties in the five high schools began to teach and field-test the contextual teaching methodology. These were mixed classes in run-of-the-mill, typical high schools, and no attempt was made to group the students.

The CLIC project was evaluated in the following four areas:

1. Teacher perceptions and attitudes about contextual teaching
2. Student perceptions and attitudes after experiencing contextual teaching
3. Analysis of student attendance patterns and behavior problems
4. Regular teacher evaluations of content or knowledge gains by students

The American College Testing Service (ACT) provided schools with testing instruments for possible analysis of student achievement as related to national norms. Ninth-grade students involved in the project took the ACT Explore pre- and posttest battery. Tenth-grade students in the project took the ACT Plan pre- and posttest battery, and the eleventh-grade students took the ACT Plan test battery as a pretest and the regular ACT College Entrance test as a posttest.

Since the individual school teams were allowed to decide which teachers and which classes were to be involved in the project, the end result involved 15 different classes over three grade levels. This made comparative evaluation of student achievement based on the ACT tests very difficult. Hence, the teacher evaluations of student progress and achievement are probably the most important indicators of student learning. However, based on ACT test results, with the exception of one school, the students who experienced contextual teaching did as well as, or better than, the national norms.

Summary of findings

Teachers were much more enthusiastic about contextual teaching at the end of the project than before the project. The consensus of the teachers in the contextual teaching classes was that:

1. Students tried harder and were more interested in their studies.
2. Students behaved better.
3. Absenteeism and tardiness were down.
4. Students seemed to enjoy the contextual classes more than the traditional classes.
5. Students seemed to accept more responsibility for their learning.

Teacher observations and evaluations

1. Students in the contextual classes made greater learning progress over the course of the school year than similar students in traditional classes.
2. Teaching contextually is a practical and relevant way to teach, but it is harder work for the teacher and it takes more planning time.
3. Students must be actively engaged in the learning process, which makes the contextual classroom quite

different from the typical traditional classroom, where students sit in rows and listen.

4. Lessons should be fun and connected to real-life issues, but a balance must be maintained between content and context.

5. Good contextual teaching takes more time for student learning than the time usually allotted in the typical class schedule.

6. Helping students make the connections between knowing and doing, and between one subject and another, is the heart of contextual teaching.

7. Contextual teaching relies heavily upon collaborative teamwork for teachers and for students, which requires extra planning time and longer class periods.

8. The role of the teacher changes from the one-way lecturer approach to an interactive, facilitator-of-learning approach.

9. Teachers need rich backgrounds to teach contextually, and more staff development time is needed.

Teacher recommendations

1. A project like this should cover two to three academic years rather than one year. It takes the first year just to get going. Furthermore, student achievement can be more accurately assessed over a longer period of time.

2. A common prep time is needed for contextual-learning team planning.

3. There is misunderstanding about contextual teaching among many teachers. Teaching contextually, or in an

applied manner, is not teaching different knowledge and skills, but teaching the same knowledge and skills differently.

4. Use of school principals as team leaders looks like a good idea on paper but just doesn't work very well. Principals have so many demands on their time that it is difficult for them to ensure good communication and keep the teams on course.

5. Longer blocks of class time are needed to really get students active in the process.

On the point of needing longer blocks of class time, it is interesting to note that one high school participating in the project was on a block schedule for freshmen and sophomores. A mixture of sophomores and freshmen stayed together in groups of about 100 with one teacher team for four to five hours each day. Students and teachers from this school expressed the most satisfaction with contextual teaching, and student test scores indicated the most improvement (Table 5).

Table 5. Student Test Scores for Freshmen at School with Block Scheduling

Subtest	Block School Mean	National Mean
English	15.8	14.2
Reading	17.3	14.2
Science	16.7	14.2

Student opinions

Dr. Sue Shields was the associate director of the project and served also as the staff development officer in one of the participating school districts. She completed her doctoral dissertation at Oregon State University using this project as the research foundation for her writing. In this research effort she surveyed 310 students and did an in-depth focus interview with 11 of the participating students. One word stands out from her student surveys and interviews, and that is "connections." As one student said, "You study a little of this and a little of that and nothing connects!" Two other words were often used by students: "application" and "meaning."

Student comments

Pro

1. I used to hate school and I don't dread it now.
2. I am a hands-on learner and this is great for me.
3. This makes school fun and it is easier to learn.
4. From what I am able to see, there is more interaction and stuff that you can use later.
5. I like teachers who ask questions, not the same old blah, blah, plug and chug!

> "I like teachers who ask questions, not the same old blah, blah, plug and chug."

Con

1. I like the traditional classroom better. I wonder if I am learning enough.
2. I like to listen more than participate in teams.

3. Some students in our team "goof-off" too much.

4. It is sometimes confusing.

5. I might be behind next year.

Table 6. Student Responses to Statements About Their Experiences in Contextual Classes

Agreements in order of strength from strong agreement, to agreement, to disagreement.

1. I enjoyed working with others in the contextual class and it helped me learn the subject.

2. I tried to never be late in my contextual class.

3. I made a special effort to attend all of my contextual classes.

4. I enjoyed learning in my contextual class.

5. I could really tell the difference in how we were taught in my contextual class versus other classes.

6. I think I learned more in my contextual class than if the subject had been taught in the normal way.

7. If given a choice, I would take a contextually taught class versus a normally taught class.

8. I looked forward to and enjoyed going to my contextual class.

9. The contextual approach should be used in all of my subjects.

10. I did better in my contextual class than I do in my other classes.

11. I have less interest in my other classes than in my contextual class.

12. There was no difference between my contextual class and other classes I have taken. (Disagree)

In summary, students indicated strong to general agreement in support of contextual teaching as they had experienced it. It was the conclusion of the large majority of students that they learn better if they know why a given lesson is important and when they know how to apply knowledge to real-life situations. Even though there was a considerable mix in grade levels and subject matter, students were supportive of contextual teaching by a large margin.

Works Cited

Contextual Learning Institute and Consortium, "Project Final Report." Oregon State University School of Education, Corvallis, Ore., 1997.

McKillip, William D., Edward J. Davis, Thomas R. Koballa Jr., and J. Steve Oliver, "A Study of *Applied Mathematics* and *Principles of Technology* Relative to the College Preparatory Curriculum Final Report." University of Georgia, July 1993.

Parnell, Dale, *Why Do I Have to Learn This?* Waco, Tex.: CORD Communications, 1995.

Secretary's Commission on Achieving Necessary Skills, United States Department of Labor, *Teaching the SCANS Competencies.* Washington, D.C.: U. S. Government Printing Office, 1992.

Shields, Sue, "A Profile of the Commonalities and Characteristics of Contextual Teaching as Practiced in Selected Educational Settings." Doctoral Dissertation, Oregon State University, Corvallis, Ore., 1997.

Sticht Thomas, *Functional Context Education—Making Learning Relevant: A Workbook.* San Diego, Calif.: Applied and Behavioral & Cognitive Sciences Inc., 1997.

Sticht, Thomas; William Armstrong, Daniel Hickey, and John Caylor, *Cast-off Youth: Policy and Training Methods from the Military Experience.* New York: Praeger Publishers, 1987.

Todd, Candace, "A Report on the Attainment of Algebra 1 Skills by Completers of *Applied Mathematics 1* and *2.*" CORD, July 1993.

CHAPTER 5

EXEMPLARY CONTEXTUAL TEACHING PRACTICES IN CORE ACADEMIC SUBJECTS

It is interesting that much of a secondary school curriculum can be described as a contextual teaching program. Just think about it—music, art, drama, journalism, physical education, speech, and the career and technical education classes like business and agriculture use the contextual teaching processes of combining knowing with doing. However, in the core academic subjects of English, math, sciences, and social sciences, which all students must take, contextual teaching is not commonplace.

This chapter features a few exemplary contextual teaching practices in the core academic subjects. I have made no attempt to be comprehensive in my selection process or descriptions or to suggest that these are the best exemplary practices to be found. Rather, I'm presenting the featured programs as representative of growing interest in contextual teaching by teachers in the core academic subjects.

Language Arts

Kentucky

Patty Arnall, an English teacher at Christian County High School in Hopkinsville, observes that overlooking the tremendous benefits of contextual teaching was the result of her training. "It took me 20 years of teaching to have the student question, 'Why do I have to learn this?' really bother me. In my teacher education program, everything was so theoretical with very little hands-on activity. . . . So there I am teaching my students in the same way that I had been taught."

In 1996 Christian County High School established an Agriculture Academy and Arnall volunteered to teach its English classes. Since there were no guidelines for teaching English to agriculture and agribusiness students, Arnall blazed her own trail by trial and error. She wanted her literature studies to connect with the students, so she chose selections about rural life like Robert Newton Peck's *A Day No Pigs Would Die* and *Broken Heartland: The Rise of America's Rural Ghetto* by Osha Gray Davidson. Class discussions were steered toward politics and the ways government policies and regulations can impact agriculture and agribusiness. Arnall asked her students to work particularly on improving their communication skills. Class assignments included work on writing projects that included such real-life subjects as advertising and public relations.

Her enthusiasm for contextual teaching is so great that she is now using contextual teaching in all her classes.

What is so alarming about the Arnall observation is that, with an exception here and there, teacher education programs still pay little attention to training teachers to teach contextually. Generally, under current circumstances, training teachers in the art of contextual teaching and understanding the way the brain works when we try to learn something is an experience that is available only as in-service.

Florida

Beth and Chip Avery, who teach English in Poinciana High School and Gateway High School respectively, in Kissimmee, have become ardent advocates of contextual teaching. They believe that applied learning can bring life and meaning to the study of literature and language arts. Beth uses poetry such as Langston Hughes's "Dreams" and "Dreams Deferred" to help students analyze their goals and interests. Students then write letters of interest, resumes, and job applications. They also write about how the personal information in these letters might change in 10 years.

The Averys indicate that the biggest challenge in contextual teaching is to maintain the proper balance between the study of content and the application of context. "We want our students to always get the knowledge they need, but with the application of that knowledge to some real-life situations, so they can retain that learning for future problem-solving situations."

New York

Donna Murano, an English teacher, and Ed Brady, a technology teacher, at Olympia High School in Rochester have integrated a junior English course with an automation robotics project. The students work in teams of two to research, design, and write about "pick-and-place" robots. With partners, students are required to construct hydraulic pick-and-place robots that can move an object from one point to another using given materials and their own creativity. The students keep daily logs of progress and compile research papers about the project; the papers include charts and graphs.

The research papers are evaluated for their content, accuracy, thoroughness, development of ideas, use of research materials, organization, documentation of ideas, and mechanics such as spelling, vocabulary, and sentence structure. The project gives students an integrated experience involving other subject matter such as math, physics, and technology as well as practice in using their writing and research skills. This project also gives students the experience of working with others and managing their time and material resources.

New York City Technical College

English faculty members at the New York City Technical College have developed highly effective "Great Thinkers" courses. These are one-semester courses offered to high school seniors for high school and college credit. The courses are team-taught by high school and college faculty on the college campus on Saturday mornings for three hours. Thus far, two theme-centered models have been developed: "Great Thinkers in Science" (e.g., Galileo, Darwin, Freud) and "Great Thinkers in Industry" (e.g., Ford, Taylor, Demming).

Each great thinker is explored through writing assignments, guest lecturers, discussions, and readings. For example, Galileo is explored through a whole class reading of the Brecht play *Galileo*. Also, group projects are completed and presentations are made to panels of high school and college teachers.

The Saturday morning time block allows flexibility for field trips and extended lab experiences. The college setting offers students access to state-of-the-art equipment and facilities. The second half of each class period is devoted to group projects related to how a key concept of a great thinker can be applied to a real-life situation. The major feature of the "Great Thinkers" course is contextual teaching, which integrates academic and technical education wherever possible.

Oregon

Doug Dickston, an instructor of English at Mt. Hood Community College in Gresham, has transformed his classrooms with a unique contextual approach to the teaching of writing. He assigns each of his English composition students a pen pal in another English composition class. Each week the students write letters to their pen pals, whom they have never met. Dickston delivers the letters.

Dickston indicates that the pen-pal strategy gives the students exposure to real-life communication problems and solutions. A student trying to decipher a confusing statement from a pen pal gains an appreciation of the usage of clear language. This exercise also gives the instructor a wonderful teaching moment as he helps the receiving pen pal develop clear questions to resolve the confusion. Dickston reports that his students work harder to make their writing clear to their pen pals than they would in the typical English class.

Most of the pen-pal letters hold great interest for their recipients because the letters are candid and based on the real-life events of real people. Dickston has discovered that all his students—regardless of age, gender, or ethnicity—learn to understand each other a little more, while acquiring valuable communication skills. But, most important, the project enables Dickston to inject meaning into the normal classroom without using extra time.

Washington

Tacoma Community College in Tacoma offers an interdisciplinary college course called "Rethinking the Future," under the leadership of Professors Bob Thaden and John Geubtner. Although content from several other disciplines finds its way into "Rethinking the Future," the disciplines of English and business give the course a basic foundation of content and context. This interdisciplinary course's purpose is to help students see the connections between business concepts and oral and written communication. Students learn college-level outlining skills and how to apply paragraph-writing techniques to business issues.

Ten college credits can be earned for completion of the course, which runs two hours per day for five days a week. Class enrollment is limited to fifty students per quarter. The course is designed to help students:

- understand the connections between disciplines that cross several subject matter boundaries,

- enjoy an interactive and contextual learning experience,
- integrate course content with the context of writing skills, and
- improve their ability to inquire and think analytically.

No textbooks are used in this course. Instead, students are encouraged to read local newspapers, special columnists' writings, and editorials from, for example, the *Wall Street Journal*. Students are encouraged to test hypotheses, explore alternatives, and develop their own conclusions.

The evaluation of this course has been positive. Faculty members indicate that students are more turned on to learning and actually learn more than when courses are taught independently. In fact, other faculty members have become enthusiastic about interdisciplinary and contextual teaching and are testing the water in other disciplines.

Mathematics

Texas

In 1998 the Waco Independent School District decided to do something to better meet the needs of middle school students who were at risk of dropping out of school. These were students with weak mathematics skills and poor performance on the Texas Assessment of Academic Skills (TAAS—a mandatory annual test). With the help of the CORD staff, a contextual "Mathematics for At-Risk Students" (MARS) program was developed.

Pilot versions of the MARS contextual teaching program were used in the 1998–1999 school year with 55 seventh- and eighth-grade at-risk students. Eighty-two comparable students formed the control group, which experienced traditional methods and materials. At the end of the school year, the MARS group of students had significantly higher TAAS scores than the control group. The teachers using the MARS contextual teaching approaches also observed improvements in student discipline and attitudes.

What is most interesting about this pilot program in the contextual teaching of mathematics for middle school students is that, of the MARS students returning to the pilot school the next fall, none required remediation. These students had retained the learning gained in the previous year.

During the 1999–2000 school year, eleven teachers in five states experimented with contextual teaching using the MARS materials with considerable success. The pretest scores for the MARS classes and the control classes were nearly the same at the beginning of the year, but the posttest scores were significantly higher for the MARS students.[1]

California

Larry Fernandez, a mathematics instructor at Sweetwater High School in National City, spent several years searching for an approach to teaching the kind of algebra and geometry that students could apply to real-world situations. Then he became a point person to use and evaluate the two-year *CORD Applied Mathematics* curriculum. As a true professional, he wanted to be accountable for a good evaluation, so he chose two test instruments to evaluate

---

[1] CCI Publishing has published the first three modules of the MARS materials under the title *Math That Works.*

student achievement: the Stanford Test and the University of California Diagnostic Readiness Tests.

Traditional and applied classes were tested. The traditional classes enrolled the upper one-third of the college-bound students, while the applied classes enrolled the middle 50 percent of the student body. The testing results were consistent over a two-year period. Traditional math classes exhibited a higher average level of math competency at the beginning of the school year. Applied math students equaled or, in most cases, surpassed the traditional students at the end of the school year.

Mathematics instructors at the local Southwestern Community College were pleased with the results of the high school applied math students. Prior to the initiation of the high school applied math program, enrollment in remedial math classes was the norm. However, it is rare today for the students who experience the high school applied math to need remedial math at the college level.

Fernandez is enthusiastic about contextual teaching in mathematics. He feels that this methodology not only increases student achievement, but also makes math meaningful for a host of students who traditionally have tuned out and dropped out of math at the earliest opportunity.

Missouri

Nickolyn Russell, mathematics coordinator in the Hillsboro School District, tries by way of interdisciplinary studies to convince her students that mathematics is all around them. To give students an idea of how science and mathematics are connected, she holds lab sessions. In one lab session students plant an amaryllis bulb around the second week of

November. Since the amaryllis grows quickly, students measure it at about the same time each day. Each student is asked to graph the data and find the line of best fit. That information is then used to predict the height of the plant at a given time. The amaryllis flowers around the Christmas break, and the student who is the most accurate predictor takes the plant home.

In Russell's freshman applied math class, each student is asked to plan a 2000-mile dream vacation for two. Students learn to read maps, plan routes of travel, budget for meals, price places to stay, and choose things to do and calculate how much they might cost. The beauty of this interdisciplinary project is that math is not the only learning that occurs. Students also learn geography, research skills, and communication skills. The students develop travel folders/reports and then give presentations to the class to convince them of the accuracy of their figures and to try to persuade classmates to take their trips with them.

Russell also uses an unusual interdisciplinary approach in her second-year applied mathematics course. In this class, she combines math with art appreciation. After designing and choosing color schemes, students find the points of intersection of linear and nonlinear equations using graphing calculators. Projects are created on regular 8.5 × 11 paper and then transferred to poster paper for display. Russell says students not only learn math, but also enjoy the classes.

Georgia

Pat Wilder, a mathematics teacher in Fitzgerald High School in Fitzgerald, relates her experience with contextual teaching to one student named Keith. Keith was enrolled in her ninth-

---

Contextual Teaching Works!

grade algebra I class for the second year in a row. By Thanksgiving, Wilder had about given up on Keith, and Keith had given up on learning algebra. Then Wilder discovered the *CORD Applied Mathematics* course and was assigned to teach it the following year. When she saw that one of the first names on her roll was Keith's, her heart sank. But, miracle of miracles, Keith became turned on by the contextual teaching and active learning that are features of the course. Not only did Keith no longer try to sleep in class, but he seemed to enjoy the challenges of trying to solve the real-life problems presented in *CORD Applied Mathematics*. Keith didn't just pass the course. He received an "A."

Wilder began to ponder what had made the difference for Keith. She had been his algebra teacher for two years in a row, so it had not been just her teaching. *CORD Applied Mathematics* is a challenging course, so the class was not easier. Something else was at work. Wilder concluded that contextual teaching had helped Keith make the connections between the content of math and the context of application, and all of a sudden the lights went on. Keith finally saw some of the real-life applications of mathematics. This led Wilder to wonder how many other students could have been turned on to math if only the applied math course had been available.

> **Keith finally saw some of the real-life applications of mathematics.**

Wisconsin

Mary Lindquist, former president of the National Council of Teachers of Mathematics, relates the story of a first-grade classroom in Wisconsin. While the teacher was collecting lunch money, she discovered that eight students out of 20 had brought their lunches from home that day. Here, she thought, was a teachable moment. She could let the students discover how many of them had not brought their lunches.

In a typical math lesson, students would first have been required to write 20–8 on their papers. The focus would have been on memory rather than problem solving. But this teacher wanted the students to discover the answer for themselves. Some students counted on their fingers, some used blocks, and some used toys. As could be expected, there were several answers to the lunch count problem, and each student was active. They all wanted to explain how they had arrived at their answers—before the teacher coached them through the problem.

This teacher explained that she wanted her students not only to get the right answer but also to understand the process behind getting that answer. She wanted them to see meaning in their math lessons rather than just relying on memory. Isn't that what contextual teaching is all about?

Oklahoma

Linda Graham, a mathematics teacher in Pawhuska High School in Pawhuska, collected some comments from students in her applied math classes.

I really like this class. Before I came here, I could not even do the simplest story problems. Now, you can see how much I have changed.

What I like about applied math is that I feel good when I leave this class each day.

I hated math with a passion before I took this class, and my past grades reflect it. I now know that I will use this later, and that gives math a sense of purpose for me.

The first time I heard about applied math I didn't know what to think, but now I realize that it isn't a "dummy course." I think it will benefit all of us.

Science

New Mexico

James Counce and Richard Barton, physics and mathematics teachers at Jemez Valley High School in Jemez Pueblo, report great success with contextual teaching in physics. Jemez Valley is a rural high school with a student population of about 300 in grades seven through twelve. The school population is composed of 60 percent Native Americans, 25 percent Hispanic Americans, and 15 percent Anglo Americans. This high school was selected by the New Mexico Department of Education to experiment with *Principles of Technology*, a contextual physics course.

The teachers indicate that about half of the students in the *Principles of Technology* class would never normally have taken a physics class or any other science class if they could help it. But not only did these nontraditional physics students do well, they also kept up with the rest of the class and learned a lot of physics in the process!

The lab experiments in this physics class were all based on real-life problems. Everything did not always turn out "by the book," but the students were learning as well as enjoying the study of physics. This physics course and the related contextual teaching do what educators usually only claim to do. They answer the student question, "Why do I have to learn this?"

Texas

Rob Franks, director of college Tech Prep programs in Texas, tells the story of his experience as a science teacher in a rural school just outside of Denton. He had been out of teaching for a number of years, and he knew that the way he had previously taught science did not reflect the way knowledge was applied in real-world situations. To prepare himself to get back into teaching, Franks took some graduate classes and began reading about contextual teaching, collaborative learning, and brain-based education. This prompted him to rework and contextualize his approach to teaching physical science. His first year back in teaching turned out to be a great success, with his students enjoying science more and learning more.

But the real evaluation of his contextual teaching came late in the spring semester. A young man considered to be a problem student by other teachers and school administrators came to Franks one day and asked him if he could count him absent from class that day rather than present. When Franks asked why, the student replied, "It's easier to explain being absent all day than it is to explain why I missed every class but yours!" Here was a student—considered to be a trouble maker—who was faithfully attending the one class that held some meaning for him.

> **"It's easier to explain being absent all day than it is to explain why I missed every class but yours!"**

Massachusetts

Judith Miller and Ronald Cheetham are professors in the Department of Biology and Biotechnology at Worcester Polytechnic Institute in Worcester. They had been given the task of reorganizing the introductory freshman biology course. After reviewing the canned lectures and the cookbook lab format of traditional introductory biology classes, they concluded that this kind of biology instruction differed little from traditionally taught high school biology. They summarized their findings by concluding that students in the traditional introductory college biology course participated only passively, and consequently there was little retention in learning and little stimulation of student interest. But how could they change this?

Miller and Cheetham wanted to offer students a high-quality experience that really turned them on to biology. They wanted to develop students' ability to think about biology rather than just memorizing a few facts and terms. They wanted students to be able to apply their knowledge to real-life situations. As a result of this analysis, they eliminated most lectures and lab assignments where students could be passive. They introduced major topics in the contextualized format of real problems for teams of students to solve. They introduced active student learning and cooperative team approaches. The laboratory experiences were designed so students could apply lab techniques to creative investigations, with labs open long hours for students who needed more learning time.

For homework, students were asked to begin developing questions relevant to the big project for the term—designing a closed life-support system for long-term space flight. In teams of three or four, they were to research and design such things as a nutritionally adequate diet; quantify the food-producing organisms necessary to sustain the diet; design a waste-processing facility, including microbial waste digestion; and consider interactions among pressure and gas composition and the water cycle in regulating animal and plant metabolism. There was plenty of content is this contextualized course.

In the evaluation of the "new" introductory biology course, students indicated a distinct preference for the contextual approach. Students learned factual information about as well as the students in the traditional biology course, and the retention of knowledge was much greater. Students indicated that they detested the large class lectures and often skipped them or slept through them. They much preferred the active, problem-solving, applied biology. The faculty member who teaches the sophomore cell biology course reported a significant increase in creative questioning from students who had experienced the new contextualized introductory biology.

In the evaluation of the "new" introductory biology course, students indicated a distinct preference for the contextual approach.

Alabama

One of my favorite testimonials for contextual teaching comes from Jo Ann Crow, a science teacher in Gadsden High School in Gadsden. At the end of one of her lab sessions, when she was endeavoring to bring closure to the experience,

Contextual Teaching Works!

Crow asked her class what they had learned that day. One student raised his hand and said, "I learned that I could *think* more than I thought I could." Crow feels that this really sums up the major advantage of contextual teaching, and for one day at least she was a total success as a teacher.

> **"I learned that I could *think*."**

We know from brain-based learning research that, when students can make the connections between knowledge and the application of that knowledge to something real in their lives, the knowledge will "stick" for future problem solving.

Social Sciences

Maryland

In 1992 the Maryland State Board of Education became the first in the United States to mandate service learning for high school graduation. This action was motivated by the State of Maryland Values Education Committee Report, which addressed the improvement of citizenship education. The program was developed to emphasize both knowing and doing, both learning and service, with the goal of nurturing active and engaged citizens and successful students.

To meet the state board requirements, students in Maryland must complete one of the following:

- Seventy-five hours of student service that includes preparation, action, and reflection components and, at the discretion of the local school system, may begin during the middle grades; or
- A locally designed program of student service that has been approved by the state superintendent of schools.

Most school districts decided to develop their own programs by infusing service learning into existing social studies programs. Experiential and community-based service activities are thus added to the existing curricula. Teachers track the students' hours of service and include that information in course evaluation and grades.

One of the biggest challenges in implementing this program in Maryland has been to educate parents, students, teachers, and the public about the importance of service learning and why combining knowing with doing is a valid educational method for developing citizenship knowledge and skills.

Our modern culture is locked into thinking that the only way "education" can occur is for students to sit in rows in classrooms and listen.

Civic Learning Across the Nation

An attitude study of American young people conducted by Peter Hart Research Associates in 1989 provides an interesting look at how individuals aged 15 to 24 thought about citizenship and civic learning some ten years ago. The study was commissioned by the People for the American Way organization, and it resulted in a publication entitled "Democracy's Next Generation."

Among the study findings are the following:

- When asked to describe a good citizen, most young people neglected to name any citizenship responsibilities beyond being a good friend and being honest and trustworthy. Only 12 percent of those surveyed cited voting as a basic tenet of citizenship.

- Nearly two out of three young people in the survey said they knew "very little" or "just some" about the way our government works. An overwhelming 70 percent of the individuals in the survey felt that politics and government seemed so complicated that they could not really understand what was going on.

Kids Voting USA

At about the same time the citizenship survey was conducted, three businessmen from Arizona traveled to Costa Rica on a fishing trip and caught much more than fish. They learned on the trip that voter turnout in that country reaches about 80 percent. When searching for an answer to this high voting record, they found a tradition in Costa Rica of children accompanying parents to the polling places. In that country, children learn early in their lives the importance of voting in a democracy.

When the three American fishermen came home, they continued their discussions about Costa Rican voting and formed "Kids Voting USA,"[2] with the purpose of increasing civic literacy by helping students experience civics rather than just reading about it. The curriculum was developed by practicing contextual social studies teachers and curriculum consultants. The curriculum activities model democratic practices at the classroom level through cooperative learning structures, group problem solving, and active student-centered experiences. The curriculum is called "Civics Alive."

---

[2] Information about Kids Voting USA can be obtained by writing Kids Voting USA, 398 South Mill Avenue, Suite 30, Tempe, AZ 85281.

There are two key pieces to the curriculum: an "Educators Guide" and something called "The Activities." The latter is a comprehensive series of K–12 classroom activities that are available in print or can be accessed online. The activities connect the classroom with the community, enabling students to develop knowledge through personal experience. Curriculum activities are grouped for grade levels K–2, 3–5, 6–8, and 9–12. The activities emphasize information gathering and critical decision making, with classroom activities extended to the home for discussions with parents. The activities part of the program ends with a trip to an official polling station on election day, where students cast their own ballots in a real-world voting experience.

In addition to voting and classroom activities, Kids Voting USA provides special opportunities throughout the school year. One of these is the CyberForum. On September 28, 1999, the CyberForum provided students nationwide with an opportunity to link online and create a dialogue with individuals such as U.S. Senator John McCain.

Typical classroom contextual lessons involve younger students in role-playing activities and classroom elections. Older students are involved in developing policy options and holding formal debates. Youth issues are gun control, school security, funding for public education, and similar issues. It is interesting that a student can go through 12, and sometimes 14 or 16, years of education and never know who pays for the schools or how the money is raised to support education. This not only could be a good contextual civic education lesson but might also be a good interdisciplinary lesson involving mathematics.

Junior Achievement Makes Economic Education Come Alive!

Junior Achievement (JA) is the world's largest and fastest-growing organization devoted entirely to promoting economic education.[3] JA now reaches 3.5 million students through 160 local offices across the nation, as well as one million students in other countries. JA programs are taught primarily by community volunteers. The national office is in Colorado Springs, Colorado; however, a local volunteer board of directors, made up of business, education, and civic leaders, raised local dollars to support the program and set local policy.

JA programs use age-appropriate curricula spanning grades K–12. In the elementary school, students learn about their roles as individuals, workers, and consumers. Middle and high school students learn about key economic and workforce issues. In the original JA program, students formed an after-school company under the guidance of a business consultant and sold products to try to make a profit. This is still done in many high school programs and the experience aspect of the program is still emphasized, but 98 percent of the program is now accomplished during the school day in social studies classes.

An interesting element of the JA program is the host of community volunteers who visit classes for five to twelve sessions, depending on the grade level. JA also furnishes the

---

[3] Information about Junior Achievement can be obtained from Junior Achievement Inc., One Education Way, Colorado Springs, CO 80906, 719-540-8000.

school with training for the volunteers and with curriculum materials.

The evaluation of the JA program, in terms of student achievement, reveals that at each grade level elementary school students who have experienced the JA program develop greater comprehension of economics principles than comparison groups of students. Among sixth graders, JA students score 27 percent higher in basic economic understanding than nonparticipants. On the high school level, JA students consistently surpass their non-JA peers on the Test for Economic Literacy.

First Grade and Economics Education

At this point in our discussion of economic education, I cannot resist the temptation to relate my experience with economic education in the first grade. As the Oregon Superintendent of Public Instruction, I wanted to know more about primary school education, since that was missing in my experience as an educator. I traded places for one month with a first-grade teacher in the Whitworth School in Dallas, Oregon. I had a theory that, because of their exposure to television, first graders could handle more complex issues than previously thought. So, I developed an economics lesson on goods and services and opened the class discussion with the question to the students, "Do you know what kind of work your daddy and mommy do to buy things for your family?" One little boy raised his hand and said, "My daddy gives love!" Well, I learned quickly that first graders tell all and so I was a bit reluctant to pursue that answer. But, the boy immediately followed up by saying, "My daddy is a minister." What a great description for the work of a minister! Another little boy followed that answer by saying, "I don't know what my daddy does, but my mother says that he sits on his duff all day." Again I was reluctant to follow up on that answer, but found out later that his daddy is a truck driver.

The point in telling this story is that I did find out that even first-grade students can handle relatively complex issues if the instruction is framed in a contextual way. To do this, you initiate teaching from what is known and familiar to the student, rather than the reverse.

Works Cited

Parnell, Dale, *Dateline: 2000: The New Higher Education Agenda*. Washington, D.C.: Community College Press, 1990.

People for the American Way, *Democracy's Next Generation*. Washington, D.C.: People for the American Way, 1989.

Remarks from various subject matter teachers were obtained from personal interviews or from unpublished statements collected by the staff of CCI Publishing.

> A myth still exists that some individuals work only with their heads and some work only with their hands, when modern life is a blend of both.
>
> Ernest Boyer

CHAPTER 6

CONTEXTUAL TEACHING: THE FOUNDATION

The Foundation for the College Tech Prep Program[1]

Contextual teaching forms the academic foundation for any Tech Prep program. In writing about the establishment of the Tech Prep Program in my book *The Neglected Majority*, I commented:

> The four-year 2+2 Tech Prep/Associate Degree Program is intended to run parallel with, and not replace, the current College Prep/Baccalaureate Degree Program. It will combine a common core of learning

---

[1] Information about the College Tech Prep Program and the related contextual teaching can be obtained by writing to David Bond, Director, National Tech Prep Network, P.O. Box 21689, Waco, Texas 76702-1689; by logging on to www.cord.org and clicking Networks; or by visiting the National Association for Tech Prep Leadership web site at (www.state.vt.us/educ/natpl).

and technical education, and will rest upon a foundation of basic proficiency development in mathematics, science, communications and technology—all in an applied setting, but with the tests of excellence applied to this program as well as to others.

That statement is just as true today as it was when I wrote it 16 years ago. By design, the original Tech Prep program was linked with a postsecondary experience, designed as a high school **and** college program. That is why I now call it the College Tech Prep Program, and my purposes were and are clear:

1. Help develop higher student achievement up and down the line of student academic talent

2. Develop better curricular continuity between high schools and colleges, particularly community and technical colleges

3. Move the image of the Tech Prep program away from being viewed as just another high school vocational program

In the basic design of the program and beginning with the junior year in high school, students select the College Tech Prep Program, even as they now select the College Prep/Baccalaureate Degree Program, and continue for four years in a structured and closely coordinated high school and college curriculum. The high school part of the College Tech Prep Program must dovetail with specific technical education programs at the college level.

The foundation of the College Tech Prep Program is built upon the notion of helping students develop a solid academic base in mathematics, science, communication, and

---

social sciences. But this foundational knowledge is taught in a manner that combines subject matter content with the context of application. *Remember, we are not talking about teaching different academic subject matter, but rather teaching the same academic subject matter differently.*

For the student who does not learn well with traditional and abstract teaching (and this is the majority of students), an ounce of student involvement, interest, activity, and making of connections is worth a pound of rote memorization and a ton of classroom seat time!

Remember, we are not talking about teaching different academic subject matter, but rather teaching the same academic subject matter differently.

One College Tech Prep student gave this typical response in a survey of students completing an applied mathematics class in the Clark County (Nevada) School District:

> I love this class! It's helped me learn a lot of things in a faster, easier way than any other math class I've ever been in. And it shows you where and when you can use the algebra, etc. that you have already learned—not just how to solve $x = ?$ I'd recommend it to anyone!

Southern Maine Technical College and Contextual Teaching[2]

Contextual teaching now seems to be the norm at Southern Maine Technical College (SMTC), in South Portland, Maine. Several years ago the members of the mathematics faculty at SMTC felt that they must help more students be successful in mathematics. They approached the college vice president and dean, William (Bill) Warren, an old friend of mine. Math classes at SMTC were the traditional college "chalk and talk," fifty-minute class sessions, three times a week, with little or no time to work independently with students. The math faculty indicated that students did not seem to see the relevance of math, and, consequently, student achievement was not where it should be.

The entire math department indicated they were united in wanting to change the ways they were teaching in order to increase student achievement. To start, they requested funds for two of their faculty members to attend a workshop on problem-solving approaches to the teaching of mathematics. Dean Warren made a deal with them: He would enthusiastically approve their request if they would recruit two people from the technical education faculty to go the workshop with them as a team.

The four faculty members completed the workshop and returned to the college with the mission of revising the mathematics curriculum and their teaching methodology

---

[2] For information about this program contact William Warren, Executive Vice President, Southern Maine Technical College, Fort Road, South Portland, Maine 04106.

Contextual Teaching Works!

along the lines of contextual teaching. The technical education instructors provided the context and the math instructors provided the math content.

During the summer of 1994, the math faculty members developed new syllabi for three basic college math courses: Foundations of Mathematics, College Algebra, and Trigonometry. Students would work in cooperative teams in two-hour class periods that, for the most part, were to be held in computer labs using new applied mathematics software called "PC: Solve." Students would assess their own learning and be assessed by others. Contextual teaching and active learning would replace the old "chalk and talk" classes. All math students would be given pre- and posttests.

The results of this first year of experimental teaching, the 1994–1995 college year, were surprising. Student feedback and suggestions were carefully evaluated, student "learning journals" were read by the faculty, and student interest and achievement in mathematics rose. Probably the best indication that the changes were working came from students who reported that they had never liked math before and were now liking it. The math faculty was particularly impressed by the fact that the weakest math students often showed the most dramatic gains in achievement.

The means of the pre- and posttest results for 1994–1995 and later years are shown in Figures 3 and 4. The pre- and posttests were standardized exams in computation and algebra; the norms used were national norms for community colleges from the Educational Testing Service, which wrote the test. Over the three academic years of the pre- and posttest study, the random sample comprised 482 students out of the several thousand taking the courses.

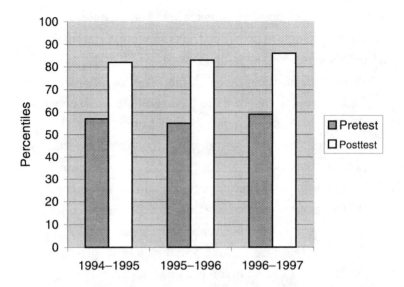

**Figure 3. Computation Pre- and
Posttest Results 1994–1997**

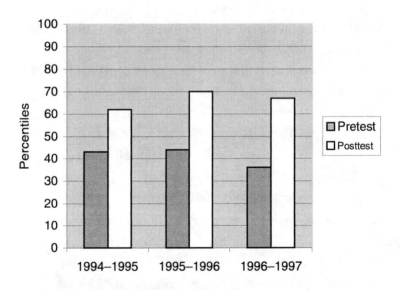

**Figure 4. Algebra Pre- and Posttest
Results 1994–1997**

Contextual Teaching Works!

Over the past few years the math faculty members have continued to improve the curriculum and their related contextual teaching. Additional services have also been developed. Faculty members meet weekly to plan and share ideas about teaching and learning. They observe each other's classes and team-teach often. They also offer noontime help sessions for students three days a week.

The enthusiasm is so high that the math instructors have reached out to the math faculty of feeder high schools. As part of this effort, the Tech Prep coordinator and the chair of the math department drafted and signed an articulation agreement that followed the *CORD Applied Mathematics* sequence for the high schools. The agreement outlines dozens of math competencies that students must demonstrate in order to request advance credit from the college. The agreement also explains in detail exactly what is taught in the college math program.

The enthusiasm is so high that the math instructors have reached out to the math faculty of feeder high schools.

The face-to-face conversations that have taken place between college and high school math instructors give good information about the math standards of the college. They also help everyone understand how to better prepare their students for success at the college.

Warren reports that this experience has impacted the culture of the college, which now follows the four "A's" of contextual teaching outlined in my book *Why Do I Have to*

Learn This?[3] The curriculum of the college and the related teaching emphasize the Acquisition of knowledge, the Application of knowledge, the Assimilation of learning, and the Association of learning for future problem solving.

The Boeing Company and Contextual Teaching[4]

The Boeing Company in Seattle, Washington, has become so convinced that contextual teaching will produce higher student achievement that this huge corporation has invested over $6 million in the schools and community colleges of the Greater Seattle area. This investment goes to train teachers in what Boeing called applied academics, and we now call the contextual teaching methodology. The effort began in the late 1980s when the Boeing Company conducted several studies of the competencies of their job applicants and entry-level workers. They found a sizable mismatch between the needs of a high-performance organization and the competencies applicants were bringing to the jobs. Most applicants showed deficiencies in mathematics, communication skills, problem-solving skills, and the ability to apply knowledge.

---

[3] Dale Parnell, *Why Do I Have to Learn This?* Waco, Tex.: CORD Communications, Inc. (now CCI Publishing), 1995.

[4] Information about evaluations of the Boeing Tech Prep and Applied Academics Program can be obtained by writing to Northwest Regional Educational Laboratory, The Boeing Tech Prep and Applied Academics Evaluation, 101 S. W. Main, Suite 500, Portland, Oregon 97204; or by writing to Lynn Brown, Tech Prep Manager, The Boeing Company, P.O. Box 3707 MC 2R-29, Seattle, Washington 93124-2207.

In response to these studies, in 1990 the company established a task force to meet with educational leaders to determine how the nation's largest aerospace corporation might help schools and colleges better prepare students for the high-tech workplace. The task force concluded that the best thing the Boeing Company could do would be to offer dollars to educational organizations to help develop applied academics courses and to train teachers in how to teach contextually. The company's executive officers agreed that a significant investment of company profits in contextual teaching and the development of applied academics courses would not only have a long-term payoff for Boeing, but would also benefit its suppliers and other employers throughout the region.

Since then, many high schools and community colleges across the Northwest have been the beneficiaries of Boeing dollars aimed at training teachers to teach contextually and to integrate academics with vocational education. Summer teacher internships in the Boeing Company have helped many teachers to overhaul courses and develop contextual learning modules.

The Boeing investment in contextual education has worked so well that the company initiated a College Tech Prep Student Internship program in 1993. Selected students committed themselves to a four-year sequence of study combining two years of high school and two years of community college and ending in an associate degree in manufacturing technology, as well as in engineering technology.

The key component of the College Tech Prep Internship is a six-week paid internship program in the Boeing Company. This takes place over three summers: between the high school junior and senior years, between the senior high school year and the first year in the community college, and between the freshman and sophomore years in the community college. During these summer experiences the students apply what they have been studying during the school year. About 500 students are now involved in the summer experience, which involves both Boeing and Boeing suppliers. The community colleges of the Greater Seattle region have agreed to grant 15 quarter-hours of college credit toward an associate degree to any student who successfully completes the three summer internships.

Another interesting aspect of the summer internship is that it lengthens the school year at little cost to the schools. However, the program does require an unusually close curricular relationship among the high schools, community colleges, and Boeing. This is a good example of bringing content and context together and providing students with much-needed experience.

Think what it might mean if nearly every employer in the country offered a structured summer internship that was closely coordinated with the curricula of the schools and colleges in its area.

Most high school and college students work during the summers anyway, but that work is not often connected to the students' education in any meaningful way. Furthermore, participating in

Think what it might mean if nearly every employer in the country offered a structured summer internship that was closely coordinated with the curriculum of the schools and colleges in its area.

Contextual Teaching Works!

the internship over a three-summer period gives the students a sense of continuity between their high school and college programs. Even a small employer could take one or two students, and public employers, like school districts or community colleges, could take many more. What prevents their participation in an internship program that prepares prospective teachers or teacher assistants? Making the employer community a full working partner in the education process would provide students with an education rich in both information and experience.

The Automotive Industry and Contextual Teaching

Fortunately, an increasing number of employers are ready to work with schools and colleges to develop Tech Prep internships related to the schools' educational programs. Beginning with the leadership of Jack Smith, president of General Motors, and now involving nearly all the leaders of the major automotive manufacturers, an organization was initiated in 1995 called Automotive Youth Educational Systems (AYES).[5] The purpose of this organization is to interest more students in pursuing careers in the automotive industry. To do this, AYES hopes to involve dealer associations and local auto dealers across the country in offering summer internships in their dealerships. The internships are established to give high school and community college students experiences that are closely tied

---

[5] Information about AYES can be obtained by writing to Don Gray, President, AYES, 2701 Troy Center Dr., Suite 450, Troy, Michigan 48084, or by visiting AYES on the web at www.ayes.org.

to the school curriculum, bringing content and context together in the workplace.

AYES involves some 150 high schools and colleges in 25 states. Nearly 1,100 local dealerships and over 1,000 master technician mentors are working with nearly 1,500 students across the nation, which is outstanding for a four-year effort. Don Gray, president and chief executive officer of AYES and long-time General Motors executive, indicates that the future looks bright for the program. It is extending the learning period for many students and improving their achievement.

Several aspects of the program are noteworthy, especially its emphasis on contextual teaching and related applied academics curriculum in the schools and its extensive Technician Mentor Training Program. Without mentor training, a master technician cannot participate in the summer internship program.

Nothing strengthens a local AYES partnership more than an exemplary summer experience for the student. Four significant quality-control elements of the summer experience contribute to student success:

1. The school appoints a coordinator for the program who is required to visit each participating dealership at least once every two weeks. During this visit, the coordinator is required to meet separately with the student, the mentor, and the service manager to check on progress.

2. Students maintain work journals to record their work experiences and confirm how these experiences relate to their school experiences.

3. Mentors and the coordinator update students' AYES Career Passports twice during the summer.

---

4. A local AYES advisory council marks the end of the successful internship with a special-event celebration for students, parents, mentors, dealership employees, and school officials.

The High Schools That Work *Program and* Contextual Teaching

The Southern Regional Education Board's *High Schools That Work* (HSTW) program is now the largest and one of the most successful education reform efforts in the nation. The major purpose of this initiative is to integrate academic and vocational education and thereby raise student achievement for all high school students. Established in 1987 under the leadership of Dr. Gene Bottoms, HSTW has grown from 28 pilot sites in 13 southern states to nearly 1,100 high schools in 23 states nationwide.

HSTW members are asked to implement the following 10 key practices for changing how students are taught, what they are taught, and what is expected of them:[6]

1. Increase student access to challenging integrated academic and vocational-technical education studies with major emphasis on improving problem-solving

---

[6] The ten practices paraphrased here form a good framework for describing an exemplary contextual teaching program. Further information can be obtained by sending for the following publication: "Finishing the Job: Improving the Achievement of Vocational Students," by Gene Bottoms and Alice Presson, Southern Regional Education Board, 592 10th, NW, Atlanta, Georgia 30318.

skills used in the modern workplace (contextual teaching).

2. Increase student access to academic studies that teach the essential concepts from the college prep curriculum by encouraging teachers and students to bring academic content together with the context of real-world problems and projects (contextual teaching).

3. Get students actively engaged in rigorous and challenging learning (contextual teaching).

4. Set high expectations for students and help them meet those expectations (contextual teaching).

5. Give students and their parents the choice of a system that integrates school-based and work-based learning over the span of high school and postsecondary education that involves educators, employers, and employees in the planning (experience-rich and information-rich teaching).

6. Develop an organizational structure and a schedule that give vocational and academic teachers time to plan and deliver integrated academic and technical education content and context (contextual teaching).

7. Have students complete a challenging program of study with an upgraded academic core and a major (contextual teaching).

8. Involve each student and his or her parents in a guidance system that ensures completion of an accelerated program of study involving an academic or a vocational-technical education major (contextual teaching).

9. Provide a structured system of extra help—and extra time—to enable students who may lack adequate

preparation to complete an accelerated program (contextual teaching).

10. Use student assessment and program evaluation data to continuously improve the school climate, organization, management, curricula, and instruction to improve student achievement and to recognize students who meet both curriculum and performance goals (contextual teaching).

An Award of Educational Achievement recognizes the efforts of students who meet the HSTW curriculum and achievement goals. Nearly 8,000 students (one-fourth of the students completing career concentrations at HSTW sites) earned the award in 1998. These students also had average achievement scores that exceeded those of college prep students, as indicated in Table 7.

Table 7. A Comparison of 1998 NAEP Scores for HSTW Award Recipients and College Prep Students[7]

	Reading	Mathematics	Science
HSTW Award Recipients	304	325	319
College Prep Control Group	302	317	307

Note: The college prep control group consists of twelfth graders who took the National Assessment of Educational Progress exams and indicated they were pursuing a college prep curriculum.

---

[7] Gene Bottoms and Alice Presson, "Finishing the Job: Improving the Achievement of Vocational Students," Atlanta, Ga.: SREB, 1999, p. 21.

HSTW was ranked one of the top three education reform models by the American Institutes for Research in 1999. The study was commissioned by five leading education associations: the National Education Association, the American Federation of Teachers, the American Association of School Administrators, the National Association of Secondary School Principals, and the National Association of Elementary School Principals. Its results were published in "An Educators Guide to School-wide Reform."

The HSTW program encourages member schools to use project-based learning to raise student achievement by getting students to complete challenging real-life projects. The projects must be based on problems that are meaningful to the students and that challenge them to acquire and apply knowledge related to several disciplines.

Project-based Learning

Project-based learning is one way to implement contextual teaching and learning. Its key strategy is connecting subject matter content with the context of application by having students solve problems, design products, improve systems, and/or organize events that pertain to real-life functions and activities.

For example, in 1995 Forest High School in Ocala, Florida, established a school within a school called the "Academy for Engineering and Manufacturing."[8] The academy involves students in grades nine through twelve

---

[8] Information on this program can be obtained by writing to Craig Ham, Director, Engineering and Manufacturing Institute of Technology, 1614 SE King St., Ocala, Florida 34471-2599.

who prepare for a cluster of careers in engineering, drafting and design, and manufacturing processes. All students complete their core academic subjects in the academy. They also take courses such as applied engineering technology and applied physics to prepare for postsecondary study.

Integrated project-based learning is the key teaching method used in the academy. Students work on both team and individual requirements as part of project activities, which combine concepts from communication, mathematics, social sciences, and technologies. Each project includes a team presentation in which students are evaluated on content, accuracy, completeness, delivery, visual aids, time management, and dress.

The program has been very successful, with 100 percent of the academy students passing the high school competency test required for graduation from Florida high schools. Also, teams of students from the academy have won several national honors including the academic knowledge bowl competition sponsored by SKILLS USA, formerly the Vocational Industrial Clubs of America (VICA).

Another type of project-based learning program can be found in Great Bend High School in Great Bend, Kansas. The "In-House Training for Business and Computers Program" is a class for high school seniors doing projects for community organizations as well as for individuals.[9] Now in its seventh year of operation, the class has developed a reputation for quality and excellence in doing such projects

---

[9] Information about this project can be obtained by writing to Grace McNaney or Kevin House, Business Education Teachers, Great Bend High School, 2027 Morton Street, Great Bend, Kansas 67530.

as making business cards and forms, developing programs for drama productions and musicals, producing a recipe book, and developing an HSTW brochure.

Students solve problems by doing the assigned work, by focusing on customer satisfaction, and by developing new computer and design skills and academic knowledge as needed to complete a job. Students fill out weekly time sheets; there are no excused absences, only reasons for being absent. Students make up lost time by working on projects before or after school. If a customer finds a mistake, the student must redo the project on his or her own time.

Before being admitted to the class, students sign contracts that outline such expectations as demonstrating a code of personal honor based on courtesy, integrity, common sense, and respect for others. Confidentiality about customer work is considered one of the class essentials. Grades are based on total time spent on projects, on productivity, and on confidential customer evaluations. Evaluations of this program indicate that students not only gain much core knowledge, but also learn how to apply that knowledge in real-life situations, making graduates of the program highly employable.

> **Before being admitted to the class, students sign contracts that outline such expectations as demonstrating a code of personal honor based on courtesy, integrity, common sense, and respect for others.**

The British Columbia Center for Applied Academics

In 1988, the Canadian province of British Columbia experienced the same close scrutiny of its schools as its U.S. counterparts. The Sullivan Royal Commission on Education Report emphasized the importance of making schooling more closely connected to the real-life career goals of students. An important recommendation in this report was that the majority of students would learn more if the curriculum were taught in the context of real-world problems.

Begun in 1996 as an experimental program, the British Columbia Center for Applied Academics was given the mandate of promoting, supporting, and assisting in the development of applied academics courses and the related teaching methodologies that we call contextual teaching.[10] The center was developed as a unique way to bridge the gap between the rules and regulations of the Ministry of Education and the educational system of the province.

Since 1996, many applied academics courses, such as applications of mathematics, applications of physics and technology, information technology, and professional communications, have been developed in British Columbia. In the 1995–1996 school year, there were only four applied academics course completions across the province. In the

---

[10] For further information about this program write to Career and Applied Programs, Curriculum Branch, Ministry of Education, P.O. Box 9152, STN PROV GOVT, Victoria, British Columbia, Canada V8W 9HI.

1998–1999 school year, there were 12,000 course completions.

Student evaluations indicate higher student achievement and a lower number of high school dropouts. As a result of the continuing success with students who have experienced the applied academics courses, most of the postsecondary institutions across the province now accept applied academics course credits for entry into their college programs.

Four Areas of Competency

Action research in British Columbia has concluded that there are at least four areas of competency that students gain from contextual teaching and applied academics programs:

1. Academic skills, such as
   - enhanced communication skills
   - technical writing skills
   - computer skills
   - mathematical skills, and
   - technology skills

2. Critical thinking skills, such as
   - hands-on problem-solving skills
   - decision-making skills, and
   - accessing, evaluating, and using information

3. Personal management skills, such as
   - positive attitude toward lifelong learning
   - confidence and self-esteem, and
   - creativity

4. Teamwork skills, such as
   - planning and making decisions with others
   - working collaboratively on projects
   - exercising give and take to achieve group results, and
   - group goal setting

The Applied Academics Center has been so successful that the Minister of Education has declared that the program is no longer experimental. It has been moved into the regular Curriculum Branch of the Ministry, under the title of the Career and Applied Programs Unit.

Contact Notes

David Bond, Director
National Tech Prep Network
P.O. Box 21689
Waco, TX 76702-1689

Gene Bottoms, Vice President
Southern Regional Education Board
592 10th Street, NW
Atlanta, Georgia 30318

Lynn Brown
Tech Prep Manager
The Boeing Company
Box 3707, MC 2R-29
Seattle, WA 98124-2207

Career and Applied Programs
Curriculum Branch, Ministry of Education
P.O. Box 91552, STN PROV GOVT
Victoria, British Columbia, Canada V8W 9HI

Don Gray, President
Automotive Youth Educational Systems
2701 Troy Center, Suite 450
Troy, MI 48084

Craig Ham, Director
Engineering and Manufacturing Institute of Technology
1614 SE King Street
Ocala, FL 34471-2599

Larry McClure, Director
Career and School to Work Programs
 Northwest Regional Educational Laboratory
101 SW Main, Suite 500
Portland, OR 97204

Grace McNaney
Business Education Department
Great Bend High School
2027 Morton St.
Great Bend, KS 67530

William Warren
Southern Maine Technical College
Fort Road
South Portland, ME 04106

> Simply placing students in a real-world context does not guarantee a learning experience. Effective contextual learning results from a complex interaction of teaching methods, content, situations, and timing.
>
> Elaine Sullivan, Ed.D.
> 1998 NAASP/MET Life Principal of the Year

CHAPTER 7

THE NEW EDUCATION AGENDA

I make no apology for my deep belief that public education is the glue that holds our very diverse country together. Where else in our land do individuals of all socioeconomic backgrounds and cultures meet on a daily basis? The almost daily drumming away about the problems of the public school system ignores the tremendous assignment that has been given to public education. I do not want to suggest that public education can solve every social ill in our culture. After all, schools

> **Public education is the glue that holds our very diverse country together.**

are but a reflection of the communities they serve, and schools have a difficult time rising above the cultures that support them. But to blame schools for "the rising ride of mediocrity," as was stated in the famous "Nation at Risk" report, is to confuse the symptoms with the disease.

In the debate about the quality of public education, we must do more than compare our schools with the agendas of the past; we must view our schools through the planning of an agenda for the future. To load public education with new

---

demands and new student populations without upgrading the schools and changing our teaching methodologies will only promote another, more subtle, type of discrimination.

By ignoring the learning needs of the neglected majority of students who have practical intelligence and who learn better with contextual teaching, we undermine public confidence in the very institutions that keep our country glued together. The new agenda must include helping *all* students raise their levels of learning achievement. This will not be accomplished by doing more of the same, with a single definition of excellence.

The world has changed, and quality education in this new century means preparing students in new ways. It seems as if many parents and observers of the educational scene have only a single definition of excellence in education: the college prep-baccalaureate degree curriculum and the related theoretical teaching that undergirds much of the public middle school and high school curriculum. Even though only about 25 percent of the public school student population will ever earn four-year college degrees, many students are made to feel that, if they are not on the road to this single definition of excellence, they are somehow second rate.

In the fall of the year 2000, a record 53 million students were enrolled in the elementary and secondary schools of the nation, mostly public schools. Our public schools have successfully met a host of new demands and now serve more students from different racial, cultural, social, and language backgrounds than ever in our history. The schools have had to respond in many instances to enrollment increases on the one hand and budget cuts on the other hand.

Public schools now educate a vast number of handicapped students who previously were shut out of public education. While admirable, this has driven up the costs of education in ways the public does not really understand. For example, it is not uncommon for a teacher's aide to be assigned to take care of a severely handicapped student in a one-on-one situation throughout the school day. The cost of this special education program is high, but the public schools have worked miracles in the service of handicapped individuals.

In an effort to help us understand what a public school teacher faces every day in a modern classroom, or what a school administrator faces every day in managing a public school, I interviewed a few teachers and administrators serving at all levels of public education to give us a reality check about the current situation in our public schools.

A Veteran Elementary School Teacher's View

I teach third grade in an elementary school that serves a basically middle class community. In my 18 years of teaching, I have seen many changes in the student population. There is a greater diversity of students today than ever before in my teaching experience, and it is a real challenge for me to meet that diversity with different teaching styles. I love my students, particularly because of their diversity, and it is so satisfying to see them grow and really learn.

My third-grade students need more "hands-on" teaching and learning today than I have experienced in the past. The great majority of my students learn better when my teaching is tied to real-world issues.

My students do not really have much of a concept about time or history. They are more "here-

and-now" learners, and are easily distracted. As an example, on President's Day in February, I was trying to help my students get some kind of an idea about President Abraham Lincoln and what he did for our country. A Korean student in my class raised his hand and asked, "Teacher, were you teaching when Mr. Lincoln was President?"

> My students do not really have much of a concept about time or history. They are more "here-and-now" learners, and are easily distracted.

I can identify in the third grade the "at-risk" and the "at-hope" students. That judgment is based upon their ability to read. Inability to read reasonably well at the end of the third grade signals future educational difficulties for a student. I think schools must pay whatever price is necessary to help kids to read while they are still in the primary grades.

Depending on the year, one-third to one-half of my students come from single-parent or blended-parent homes, which often limits the amount of time a parent can spend in helping with the child's education. One out of

> Inability to read reasonably well at the end of the third grade signals future educational difficulties for a student.

every five or six of my students comes from a home where the use of alcohol is problematic, and that really creates problems for the child. It seems that I have only two kinds of parents of my students. About half of my parents have healthy involvement with their children and with the schools; the other half have either unhealthy or sparse involvement with their children and the school.

One of the joys of teaching in a self-contained classroom is that my teaching is not tied to a 55-minute learning period, as it is in the high schools. I can usually take whatever time is needed for my students to master learning. This helps me to be a student-centered teacher rather than a subject-centered teacher. It is also important to keep class sizes relatively small in the primary grades because I try very hard to really get to know my students, concentrating on how they learn best and then tailoring my teaching to match that learning style.

My final observation about the changes I have seen in public education has to do with the goals and purposes of my school district. It seems that there is a continuing flow of new demands made on our schools. I am beginning to wonder where that stops and when new attention and priority will be given to what happens in the classroom.

*   *   *

A Middle School Counselor Speaks Out

When I walk into my school at 7 A.M., I always expect the unexpected. There are new surprises every day. Some of the surprises are wonderful, and an increasing number of the surprises are not so wonderful. We have students from wealthy homes; we have students who move from school to school; we have many students who come from solid middle class homes; we have a large number of handicapped and special education students; and we have students who are temporarily homeless and living out of cars. This is my 20th year of teaching and counseling in the middle school, and I have seen many changes in how we operate our schools, many of which are results of the breakdown of family life and the home.

It seems that there are so many new demands on our schools that I wonder if teaching and learning are still our major purpose. We must worry about who qualifies for free lunches and argue with some parents about this. We operate a clothes closet to give out shoes, coats, and backpacks to those who cannot afford these items. We worry about students getting their immunization shots and about other health matters. When some individual students consistently come to school with bruises on their arms and legs, we worry that these students may need help.

As a counselor, I spend a lot of time dealing with psychological problems that arise from divorce, split homes, abusive homes, and the use of drugs. School safety is another new issue that requires constant vigilance. For some kids, school teachers and counselors are about the only parents that they know. Since I am the only counselor in a school of 800 students, most of my time is spent dealing with emergencies such as the grief when a sixth-grade boy hanged himself at home, suffering from the effects of an abusive stepfather.

> As a counselor, I spend a lot of time dealing with psychological problems that arise from divorce, split homes, abusive homes, and the use of drugs.

One of the recent and time-consuming demands is for more testing. It seems that much of the impetus for testing comes from political sources rather than from educational sources. I really wonder if all the time and money spent on standardized testing lead to a true assessment of the quality of teaching and learning going on in our school. In my judgment, reading and writing are taught best by having our students read and write about meaningful things, rather than spending a lot of time preparing students for some arbitrary test through meaningless rote memorization exercises.

Thank goodness for good and dedicated teachers and a principal who really cares about kids. I am also thankful for some of our success stories. For example, three of our 14-year-old girls were caught smoking in the middle of our school campus. When they were referred to me for counseling, I met every week with them, reviewing their assigned research. This I had worked out with their language arts teacher, and it involved researching the health issues involved in smoking. By the end of the school year, these three girls were making presentations to fifth graders at nearby elementary schools about the health hazards involved with smoking. As a result of this real-life experience, I saw behavior changes for the better and school grades going up.

*   *   *

A High School Vice Principal Reflects

The biggest change I have seen impacting our school has been the change in family life. This spills over into the school in several ways. Many single parents are working hard just to survive, much less to be involved in the school life of their students. In handling discipline problems, I have some parents tell me they just do not know what to do with their kids and they ask if I can help discipline them.

In many cases, the schools have become surrogate parents for students. It seems that students have less direction from home today and an increasing number of parents give the schools less support. On top of that, we are a very mobile society and we have students moving into and out of our school all the time.

I have served as a school teacher and administrator for 27 years, and the problem that bothers me the most has to do with child abuse and sexual abuse, which may be related to the growing drug and alcohol abuse problem. This may have been a problem all along and is just now coming to the surface, but it seems that students are much more willing to talk about it and ask for help from the only place they can turn to for help—the school.

There is also an increasing demand for special services from the schools. In my high school, about 50 percent of our students qualify for free breakfasts and free lunches. We now operate an alternative school for those students who just are not making it in the regular school program. More and more of our students are "hands-on-learners." Special education now provides services for severely handicapped students and endeavors to mainstream these individuals into the regular school day wherever possible.

There are so many demands made on the schools, I wish we could review the goals of our school district and establish some priorities. What is our primary job?

But my observations are not all negative. Many good things are happening in our

> **I wish we could review the goals of our school district and establish some priorities.**

high school. I think the new teachers are better trained and are generally better teachers than some of the older teachers. I am seeing much more contextual teaching than ever before, and this is helping many students to gain higher levels of achievement. I hope we can get more teachers interested in that method of teaching. We have a Naval Junior ROTC in our school involving 125 to 150 students. This is a real hands-on program and it is keeping a number of kids in school who might otherwise drop out.

Many more girls are now involved in technical education programs and athletics. Our Future Farmers of America program (FFA) is now dominated by girls and is probably our most active high school club. A father of one of our most active FFA girls told me that he now knows what FFA stands for—it means Father Farms Alone. We also have a strong technical education program, but it has been difficult to get our core academic teachers interested in integrating academic with vocational education. They tend to be pretty traditional teachers.

Technology has had a positive impact on our school. Every teacher has a computer on his or her desk and there is now a telephone in every classroom. This has happened in just the last few years. Our task now is to use the technology in ways that will make a bigger impact on increasing student achievement.

*   *   *

A School District Director of Staff Development Sees Changes

Over my 29 years in teaching and public school administration, I have observed a large number of changes that impact education. Some are good and have been beneficial for the schools, but a large number have created real challenges. I always like to concentrate on the good things first, so let me start there.

Staff development has become more of a priority in recent years. Administrators and school board members are realizing that, if improvements are to be made in our schools, an investment must be made in the people who will make the improvements. Furthermore, staff development must be much more than an opening session at the beginning of the school year when the superintendent gives greetings and new teachers are introduced. It must become a year-round operation with the highest priority given to the improvement of teaching and learning.

> If improvements are to be made in our schools, an investment must be made in the people who will make the improvements.

Special education has become a priority for the public schools as a result of the federal Americans with Disabilities Act. Schools are now serving a student population that has, by and large, been previously ignored, and there are many more special services in the schools to serve these special-needs students. These services range from speech therapy, to serving the physically handicapped, to serving the mentally challenged, to serving the emotionally handicapped, to serving students with severe attention deficits, to the development of alternative schools. It is true that these services have driven up the cost of public education, but special education services have made dramatic contributions to thousands of children who would otherwise have been neglected.

I also see better teachers and better teaching than ever before. There is more contextual and project-based teaching today than at any time in the recent past. More teachers are working in teams and more are reaching out to seek partnerships in the community and with their counterparts in postsecondary education. Many students are now graduating from high school with several college credits under their belts. This not only saves them money, but gives students a push into college.

There has been significant change in the use of technology in the schools. A few years ago, you would have been hard pressed to find even one computer in the typical school. Today, technology is commonplace in the schools, with nearly every teacher having a computer at his or her desk. In the mid-1980s we were still using electric typewriters throughout our schools. Today e-mail is commonplace, and increasingly teachers are incorporating the use of technology into their teaching.

Computer devices not only are growing in number and sophistication, but are emerging as key providers of knowledge and information, which changes the role of the teacher. The teacher of today and tomorrow must be more than a knowledge giver. Modern technology has changed the role of the teacher from the knowledge bank to the person who helps students make the connections between knowledge and the application of that knowledge.

The invention of the computer has given staff development in the schools a new push and a host of new opportunities.

Changing demographics are also motivating the schools to make changes. Students are different. They have been raised on television and video games and are much more active learners than sit-and-listen learners, which requires a different teaching methodology from traditional teaching. There is also much more racial and cultural diversity in the average classroom today than 29 years ago when I began teaching. It is not uncommon today to have a half-dozen or more native languages spoken. In large urban school districts, teachers might experience as many as 40 to 50 different languages being spoken. Most noticeable in the modern classroom is the divide between the economic haves and the have-nots. The family structure, or lack of it, seems to have as much to do with student achievement as what goes on in the schools.

The political climate is also much different today from that of even a few years ago. There are many more senior citizens living on fixed incomes with no children in school who have a problem with increased property taxes to support the local schools. They are not anti-education, but for the most part they are anti-property taxes. One result of the property-tax revolt is more state-level funding and more state-level control of local schools. With more state control come more assessment demands and more state mandates. As a result, educators always seem to be

> **The political climate is also much different today from that of even a few years ago.**

on the defensive justifying their existence. Teaching and learning take a back seat most of the time to the external pressures and demands forced upon the schools.

It seems as if the schools are also expected to have joint custody of the children with the parents. Breakfast is served in the morning, lunch is served at noon, and after-school activities are served in the evenings. School safety and health issues are of greater concern. In this litigious culture, every precaution is taken in the operation of the schools to avoid lawsuits. An increasing cost of doing business in the schools has to do with legal issues, and that concern clouds much of what we do in educational administration. For many people, including teachers, the mission of the schools is not very clear. Maybe it is time to reexamine the goals and expectations of the schools.

It is an exciting time to be involved in education, but one had better be aware of the changes requiring different teaching methods and different administration and leadership styles. Doing the same old thing just won't work.

*　　　*　　　*

The New Agenda

The key in reviewing the quality of any organization is to see how well purpose, or mission, is linked with action. The modern curriculum and contemporary practices of teaching cannot be disconnected from the overall mission of schooling in the vain hope that it will all somehow connect one day for teachers and students. For schools and colleges to be effective, they must have a sense of mission that is widely shared by students, teachers, administrators, board members, parents, employers, and the community. Unless actions reflect and support the educational mission of the schools, there is little hope of effectively shaping the future of the organization. It is like a builder endeavoring to build a house from two or three different sets of blueprints.

> **The key in reviewing the quality of any organization is to see how well purpose, or mission, is linked with action.**

What Is Primary and What Is Secondary?

The first thing to accomplish in fulfilling our new agenda for education is a reexamination of the mission of our educational institutions. What is the purpose that should drive the development of goals for education? Should it be the *primary* purpose of schooling to help each student develop the competencies to function effectively as a lifelong learner, citizen, consumer, and producer or worker? If we can establish that *primary* accountability, we can then develop our mission priorities along that line and further state what we deem to be our shared and *secondary* accountabilities.

Fundamental changes in our society and in our student bodies call for corresponding shifts in our educational goals and institutional missions. A problem common to many educational goals is that they are out of date, failing to reflect societal realities and the real-life needs of a majority of our students. In many ways young people of today, and their needs, have outgrown our schools and their mission statements.

One of the key problems with educational mission statements is that they are often so vague or general that they give weak direction for teaching and curriculum development. Such statements as "pursuing excellence," "improving the condition of humankind," "producing well-educated citizens," or "leaving no child behind" may be good for political speeches but provide little guidance for the teaching and learning process.

What activities do most people have in common? While we are all different, we have similar basic needs and perform certain basic functions. Each of us functions in a variety of roles throughout a lifetime, and the requirements of these life roles present a promising beginning point for establishing educational goals, which teachers can then relate to contextual teaching. These basic functions, called "human commonality roles," can form the foundation for establishing goals with a clear view of the basic purposes of public education.

A human commonality can be described as a life role that a human being performs throughout a lifetime. It is vital to recognize that students are already living most of these roles and are experiencing them with or without developing the competencies needed to achieve a measure of success and fulfillment in the roles.

What are these human commonalities? Obviously, they can be categorized in several ways, but I have identified seven strands that run through the education curriculum as follows:

1. Citizen

2. Lifelong Learner

3. Individual or Self

4. Family Member

5. Producer or Worker

6. Aesthetic or Leisure Participant

7. Consumer

Four of the commonality strands probably represent the *primary* areas of accountability for schools. They can be worked into a mission statement by stating that it is the schools' responsibility to help students gain the knowledge and application skills (competencies), to function as lifelong learners, citizens, consumers, and producers.

> **Four of the commonality strands probably represent the *primary* areas of accountability for schools.**

Schools have a *secondary* responsibility and shared accountability with the home, church, the media, and governmental agencies to help students develop the competencies to function effectively as family members, self-knowing individuals, and individuals who have developed aesthetic appreciation for what is good, true, and beautiful. Figure 5 suggests a contextual teaching-human commonality paradigm around which an educational mission statement can be developed.

SELF	CITIZEN
• Understand and practice physical health principles • Understand and practice mental health principles • Understand and practice principles for making moral choices • Responsibility • Self-management • Integrity • Self-esteem • Developing interpersonal and intergroup skills	• Understanding responsibilities of a citizen • Understanding local and state government operations • Coping with bureaucracies • Understanding basic principles of taxes and the economy • Locating community resources • Understanding principles in the conservation of natural resources • Understanding human diversity
LEARNER	AESTHETIC AND PLEASURE
• Writing • Reading • Listening • Speaking • Arithmetic and math • Solving problems • Thinking creatively • Seeing things in the mind's eye • Critical thinking	• Developing an appreciation for the good, true, and beautiful • Developing avocational skills • Developing creative abilities • Understanding the role of recreation • Understanding and protecting the natural environment
PRODUCER	CONSUMER
• Understanding of careers • Developing salable skills • Managing money, time, and materials • Using information • Using computers • Acquiring and evaluating data • Understanding systems • Understanding organizations • Using technology	• Understanding principles of goods and services • Evaluating quantity and quality of goods and services • Understanding basic legal documents • Computing interest rates and understanding credit • Understanding insurance, annuities, savings principles • Understanding the basic economic system • Understanding business organization
FAMILY	
• Understanding social and legal responsibilities for parenting • Understanding the principles for managing finances	• Understanding family planning • Learning to deal with family crisis, i.e., death, divorce, illness, financial problems

Figure 5. The Human Commonalities Paradigm and Contextual Teaching[1]

---

[1] Dale Parnell, *Why Do I Have to Learn This?* Waco, Tex.: CORD Communications Inc., 1995, p. 46

Contextual Teaching

One of the serious problems facing modern educational organizations is a lack of congruence between the traditional subject matter disciplines and the competencies required for functioning effectively in our human commonality roles. Our daily lives simply do not fall into the neat categories of mathematics, social science, science, and English, although the knowledge and skills traditionally tied to these disparate areas certainly can be applied to the requirements for daily living.

In contextual teaching, student competence is defined as a demonstrated ability to understand and apply knowledge. Therefore, embedded deeply within the philosophy of contextual teaching is the idea that every student must have the opportunity not only to gain knowledge, but also to be able to apply that knowledge to one or more of the human commonalities or life roles. Thus, there is a profound shift in emphasis from what is to be taught to what is to be learned. This is the most basic characteristic of contextual teaching and serves as a learner-centered bridge between the subject matter disciplines and the competencies needed to function successfully in life roles. This provides a content-rich and a context-rich education.

Figure 6 shows what a sample contextual teaching lesson plan might look like.

Course Name:	Textbook or Other Resources:

What Do I Want My Students to Know?

Content:

- -

Context:

What human commonality is addressed?

Why do students need to know this?

How will I connect this content to an application?

How Will Students Learn This?

Activity: What will students do?

Strategy: How will they do it?

Time: How will I deal with those who need more than the allotted time for the activity?

Feedback and Assessment

Performance Task: How will students demonstrate that they have learned it?

**Figure 6. A Sample Contextual
Teaching Lesson Plan Guide[2]**

---

[2] Adapted from *Why Do I Have to Learn This? Workbook* by Sandra Haake Harwell, Waco, Tex.: CCI Publishing, 1999.

If we as educators are serious about increasing student achievement, we must help *all* students make the connections between classroom subject matter and the competencies they must develop to meet the challenges they will face throughout their lifetimes. Connecting the "why" of concrete reality to the teaching process will provide more students with a motivational force for learning. If higher levels of student achievement are to be reached, more students must see and feel the touchstones of reality and meaning in the educational enterprise.

Competence Must Be the Constant and Time the Variable

Our current educational system seems to sort most students on the basis of those who learn within an arbitrary time allocation and those who do not. This system is reinforced by teachers who grade on the curve, rather than on mastery, and test experts who develop norm-based standardized tests. As one school board member said with tongue-in-cheek, "Did you know that half of our students are below average?"

> Our current educational system seems to sort most students on the basis of those who learn within an arbitrary time allocation and those who do not.

The assembly-line education that exists in most sectors of education is an inherited relic of the industrial age. This has created a significant barrier to meeting the needs of an increasingly diverse student population. Any serious attempt to establish a new agenda for education that will place increasing student achievement at the center of the effort must reverse the traditional relationship between time and competence.

Concluding Thought

In this short book, I hope to engage more people in thinking critically about what the teaching and learning process should involve in our efforts to educate a diverse student population to reach higher levels of achievement. The major focus of my writing has been the advantages of contextual teaching, particularly for the neglected majority of students who do not deal well with abstractions and theoretical teaching methods.

During my 50 years in education, I have served as a high school teacher, high school principal, school superintendent, state school superintendent, community college president, and university professor. Some wags observe that it doesn't look like I could hold a job for very long; however, these experiences have given me an unusual opportunity to observe the successes and failures of various education reform efforts. I have concluded that education reform continues to work at the margins of educational institutions and organizations.

This writing has asked the fundamental question, "What happens when the instructor closes the classroom door?" The spotlight has been thrown upon how to improve achievement for more students. Thank goodness for a host of hard-working teachers and administrators who, often working under great difficulties, hold this nonsystem of education together. It appears to me that they are ready for the new agenda.

Note

The interviews with the educators in this chapter were transcribed as accurately as possible. Some paraphrasing was done to gain clarity. Participants were not identified, but they are educators in schools in Oregon and Washington.

Books on Contextual Teaching
Order Form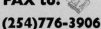

Bill to:
Name _____
Position _____
School/Organization _____
Address _____
City/State/Zip _____
Telephone ( ) _____

Ship to:
Name _____
Position _____
School/Organization _____
*Address _____
City/State/Zip _____
Telephone ( ) _____

Purchase Order No.: _____

Please include street address only.

Quantity	Title or Product Description	*Unit cost	Amount
	Contextual Teaching Works! Hardcover (Parnell)	$28.00	
	Contextual Teaching Works! Softcover (Parnell)	$16.00	
	Why Do I Have To Learn This? (Parnell)	$16.00	
	Why Do I Have To Learn This? Workbook (Harwell)	$11.95	
	Why Do I Have To Learn This? Combo (Parnell/Harwell)	$23.95	
	Opening Minds Opening Doors (Hull)	$16.00	
	Teaching Science Contextually	$3.95	
	Teaching Mathematics Contextually	$3.95	

Method of Payment:

❏ Check enclosed   ❏ PO enclosed
❏ VISA   ❏ MasterCard
❏ Discover   ❏ AMEX

Acct No. _____
Exp. Date: _____

Subtotal	
8% Shipping/Handling ($5.00 minimum)	
TX Residents add 8.25% sales tax	
Total Amount	

Prices are subject to change without notice

Mail to:

CCI Publishing
Attn: Educational Sales
P.O. Box 21206
Waco, TX 76702-1206
(800)231-3015

FAX to:

(254)776-3906
Attn: Educational Sales

C.C.I.
PUBLISHING
www.ccipublishing.com

900CTW